Bud E. Smith

Sams **Teach Yourself**

Google Places

in 10 Minutes

SAMS

800 East 96th Street, Indianapolis, Indiana 46240

Sams Teach Yourself Google Places in 10 Minutes
Copyright © 2011 by Pearson Education, Inc.

International Standard Book Number-10: 0-672-33535-2

International Standard Book Number-13: 978-0-672-33535-8

Library of Congress Cataloging-in-Publication Data is on file.

Trademarks

All terms mentioned in this book that are known to be trademarks or service marks have been appropriately capitalized. Pearson cannot attest to the accuracy of this information. Use of a term in this book should not be regarded as affecting the validity of any trademark or service mark.

Warning and Disclaimer

Every effort has been made to make this book as complete and as accurate as possible, but no warranty or fitness is implied. The information provided is on an "as is" basis. The author and the information contained in this book.

Bulk Sales

Pearson offers excellent discounts on this book when ordered in quantity for bulk purchases or special sales. For more information, please contact

> **U.S. Corporate and Government Sales**
> **1-800-382-3419**
> **corpsales@pearsontechgroup.com**

For sales outside of the U.S., please contact

> **International Sales**
> **international@pearsoned.com**

Executive Editor
Greg Wiegand

Acquisitions Editor
Rick Kughen

Development Editor
Michael Henry

Technical Editor
Karen Weinstein

Managing Editor
Sandra Schroeder

Project Editor
Mandie Frank

Copy Editor
Keith Cline

Proofreader
Water Crest Publishing

Indexer
Erika Millen

Compositor
Mark Shirar
Nonie Ratcliff

Book Designer
Gary Adair

Editorial Assistant
Cindy Teeters

Contents

About the Author

Bud Smith has written more than a dozen books about computer hardware and software, with more than a million copies sold. Bud's recent books include two from Sams: *Sams Teach Yourself Tumblr in 10 Minutes* and *Sams Teach Yourself iPad in 10 Minutes*. His other books include extensive coverage of Google, most recently including *How to Do Everything Nexus One*, *Google Business Solutions All-In-One For Dummies*, and *Google Voice For Dummies*.

Bud started out as a technical writer and journalist, and then moved into marketing and product management for technology companies. He worked at Apple Computer as a Senior Product Manager; at Google competitor AltaVista as a Group Product Manager; and at GPS navigation company Navman as a Global Product Manager.

Bud holds a BA in Information Systems Management from the University of San Francisco and an MSc in Information Systems from the London School of Economics. He currently lives in the San Francisco Bay Area, participating in environmental causes when he's not working on one of his many technology-related projects.

Dedication

This book is dedicated to you—the businesspeople, nonprofit organizers, civil servants, and others who work hard to serve the public.

Acknowledgments

Acquisitions editor Rick Kughen has been a great guide in getting this book through the collaborative decision-making and creative processes at Sams—not only intact, but improved. Project editor Mandie Frank and development editor Michael Henry steamed and straightened tangled sentences. Technical editor Karen Weinstein and copy editor Keith Cline checked all the steps and instructions to help make them clear and correct.

We Want to Hear from You

As the reader of this book, you are our most important critic and commentator. We value your opinion and want to know what we're doing right, what we could do better, what areas you'd like to see us publish in, and any other words of wisdom you're willing to pass our way.

You can email or write me directly to let me know what you did or didn't like about this book—as well as what we can do to make our books stronger.

Please note that I cannot help you with technical problems related to the topic of this book, and that due to the high volume of mail I receive, I might not be able to reply to every message.

When you write, please be sure to include this book's title and author, as well as your name and contact information. I will carefully review your comments and share them with the author and editors who worked on the book.

Email: consumer@samspublishing.com

Mail: Greg Wiegand
         Associate Publisher
         800 East 96th Street
         Indianapolis, IN 46240 USA

Introduction

Google Places is the biggest opportunity ever for locally based businesses to get online, get found, and get more new and repeat business. It's (relatively) easy to set up, easy to keep up-to-date, easy to manage, and very likely to get used in a way that brings in customers.

The tide is running in your favor, too. People want to shop locally, understanding that it's better for their communities, for the environment, and, if done carefully, for their pocketbooks. And there are more and more tools to help them to shop near their homes, workplaces, and other favored locations.

Taking advantage of these tools is the tricky bit. Owners of local businesses are responsible for what seems like a million things at once. You have to serve customers, get supplies, pay bills, and manage employees—or yourself, the most difficult employee of all! Switching gears from all this to looking after a very visible and very important online presence on Google Places might seem like too much bother.

So, Sams and I are bringing you this book to make it easier. We've broken down the steps you need to take full advantage of Google Places into a series of 10-minute lessons, each very specific and to the point.

You can get quick benefits from Google Places even if you don't have much time for it—even if you just find your business online, verify that you are the owner, and then edit the core information to make sure it's correct. You don't want an out-of-date phone number or incorrect hours to appear!

To really get the most out of Google Places, though, requires six major areas of focus:

▶ **Accurate business information:** Begin by claiming your business listing on Google. Then, as with any listing, the information you list on Google Places has to be accurate, spelled correctly, and use correct capitalization, punctuation, and grammar. This includes your business name, category of business, location, hours, and more. As the old saying goes, "You only get one chance to make a first impression," so you want to get this right and keep it current.

▶ **Photos and videos:** People want to be able to experience your business before taking the time and trouble to visit it. You must be delivering a pretty good experience or you wouldn't be able to stay in business, so you just need to share a bit of that through photos and videos. This book will show you how.

▶ **Search engine and Google Maps results:** Your business has to be able to be found, both by name, which should be easy, and by the local area and type of business ("nearby shoe stores"), which is trickier. Google Places gives you your best chance ever to help yourself be found by search engines or Google Maps, whether from a computer, tablet computer, or mobile phone. However, you still have to work at it for good results, and we show you how.

▶ **Reviews, reviews, reviews:** The stunning popularity of Yelp's local business listings in many areas just shows how badly people want review information before investing their time and money to visit your location. You need to do all you can to get plenty of good reviews, without manipulating the process. Again, this book takes you through the necessities.

▶ **Coupons and co-marketing:** Google Places makes it easy for you to create coupons and make them available online. Initially, this is great for "training" web surfers to shop locally. Over time, you can then tie this to print, in-store, and other promotions, creating a web of offers—no pun intended—to irresistibly draw in desired customers.

▶ **Websites and social media:** You've probably been told over and over that you should have at least one website and a presence on social media such as Facebook, Twitter, and newer tools, as well. Google Places gives you a whole new reason to be online in these other areas.

It's easy to see all this as a burden—but, really, it's an opportunity. It took courage, capital, and hard work for you to set up and succeed in business in the first place. Now there's a whole new way to bring your business to life and to compete with the online-only retailers who might have been eating into your targeted-customers mindshare and market share.

With Google Places, and the other tools referred to in this book, you will likely be able to achieve a lively, thriving online presence—and a lively, thriving "real" business, as well. A business ready to take on all comers, local or online.

About This Book

As part of the *Sams Teach Yourself in 10 Minutes* guides, this book aims to teach you the ins and outs of using Google Places without using up a lot of precious time. Divided into easy-to-follow lessons that you can tackle in about 10 minutes each, you learn the following Google Places tasks and topics:

- ▶ Understanding who Google Places is for

- ▶ Claiming your Google Places page

- ▶ Entering and updating your business data

- ▶ Showing up high in Google Search results

- ▶ Showing up in Google Maps searches

- ▶ Getting positive customer reviews in Google Places and elsewhere

- ▶ Adding photos to Google Places and your web page

- ▶ Adding video clips and live video to Google Places and your web page

- ▶ Adding real-time updates to your Google Places site

- ▶ Using QR codes to tell customers what you're all about

- ▶ Creating a basic business website

- ▶ Paying for tags to improve map search results

▶ Managing online impressions from your Dashboard

▶ Getting detailed feedback from your Dashboard and elsewhere

▶ Moving up to Google Adwords

After you finish these lessons, and the others in this book, you'll know all you need to know to take Google Places as far as you want it to go.

Who This Book Is For

This book is aimed at all business owners who want to create a Google Places presence or improve an existing one—which should mean just about all business owners! This includes those who have extensive computer and online experience and those who have very little. It also includes those with some experience in marketing their business through various means, including print/online media, and those with very little.

The term *business owners* is meant very broadly. If you work in a social services agency, a public facility such as a swimming pool, or a nonprofit, you have people who you might call *clients*, *customers*, or some other term. They still need to know where you are, when you're open, and what previous visitors have said about you. So, *business* means any store or service provider that's open to the public!

Each lesson in this book focuses on one specific topic, such as claiming your Google Places page or showing up in Google Maps searches. You can skip from one topic to another, read the book through from start to finish, or both. You can hand it to friends, family members, or colleagues to answer a specific question that they have, too.

What Do I Need to Use This Book?

You will need a computer with a web browser and reliable Internet access to use this book. A tablet computer, such as the iPad, or a small, low-cost netbook will probably not be adequate for the tasks needed; you will probably want either a Windows PC or a Macintosh. Either a desktop or a laptop model will do the job.

If you are not experienced with computers, or don't have a computer, you might want to buy a computer and procure Internet access, and then learn how to use the computer itself and a web browser.

Alternatively, you can find a friend or work colleague with the necessary equipment and skills and the willingness to help you carry out the tasks involved. If you are the one with the necessities, you can provide help to others; it's fun to work together on tasks such as those involved with a Google Places presence.

Conventions Used in This Book

Whenever you need to push a particular button on your computer, or click a particular control onscreen, you'll find the label or name for that item bolded in the text, such as "click the **Home** button." In addition to the text and figures in this book, you'll also encounter some special boxes labeled Tip, Note, and Caution.

> TIP: Tips offer helpful shortcuts or easier ways to do something.

> NOTE: Notes are extra bits of information related to the text that might help you expand your knowledge or understanding.

> CAUTION: Cautions are warnings or other important information you need to know about the consequences of using a feature or executing a task.

Screen Captures

The figures captured for this book come from a Windows PC running Internet Explorer 8 and show various web pages, mostly in Google Places. You can use Places on a Macintosh or a Windows PC running Windows 7, Vista, or XP.

You can use a different web browser, or a different version of Internet Explorer, and different settings for your computer and your web browser. For any of these reasons, your screens might look somewhat different from those in the book. Also keep in mind that the developers of Google Places and the software and other websites shown in this book are constantly working to improve their software, websites, and the services offered on them.

New features are added regularly to the Windows and Mac OS, software, and websites, and old ones change or disappear. This means the screen contents change often, so your own screens might differ from the ones shown in this book. Don't be too alarmed, however. The basics, although they are tweaked in appearance from time to time, stay mostly the same in principle and usage.

Introducing Google Places

In this lesson, you'll learn about the basics of Google Places: what it's for, what you'll find on a typical Google Places page, and how to use Google Places to stand out from your competitors.

Why Google Places?

There's an old, six-word formula for how to get rich: Find a need and fill it. That's what Google has done with Google Places.

What's the need, though, that Google Places fills? There are a lot of different ways to describe it, but I suggest the following is best: a Yellow Pages directory for the digital age.

People used to depend on the Yellow Pages for all sorts of things. City Yellow Page directories used to be chock-a-block full of listings, with large display ads for popular categories such as furniture or pest control, and small, type-only listings for categories that were forbidden to advertise in a showy way, such as lawyers and doctors.

With the advent of the Web about two decades ago, though, more and more people have turned to online search to find things. The Web, though, hasn't been very good at local search. At the same time, the Yellow Pages business fragmented, with more players chasing a shrinking pie. So, the need to find local businesses was not effectively filled.

Google Places pulls together information found around the Web with details entered by businesses and additional features, such as photos, and makes it all easy to search for and find. And it uses location data to make the search results much more useful.

There are some difficulties with Google Places. Support and how-to information is incomplete, and scattered around various Google and non-Google sites—but that's where this book fills in a gap. Knowing just how much effort to put into it can be tricky and depends partly on what your local, national, and online competitors are doing, so making that decision is your job as a businessperson. The final issue is finding the time to get started, but that's why this book is divided into 10-minute lessons: to make the job manageable.

> CAUTION: **Google Places Editing Not Available Everywhere**
>
> This book assumes that you are in a location where Google has enabled all editing capabilities for Google Places. However, some editing capabilities are not available in all countries. For an up-to-date view of which capabilities are available in your country, check the list at this web address:
>
> http://maps.google.com/support/bin/answer.py?hl=en&answer=16 8339.

Getting Local

Why is something like Google Places becoming popular only now, more than 20 years after the Web was invented? Much of the reason has to do with location data.

It's not obvious, when people do web search, where they're searching from. However, there are now techniques for using a computer's Internet Protocol (IP) address—its unique identifier on the Internet—to get its physical address (or the physical address of the wireless network it's connected to, which is almost as good). These services are collectively called *geolocation* services. They're not always perfectly accurate, but they do the job most of the time.

> PLAIN ENGLISH: **Geolocation**
>
> Geolocation is a fancy word for a technology that uses your cell phone or computer to determine your exact location (country, region, city, ZIP code, street address, and so on).

> CAUTION: **Your Mileage May Vary**
>
> Local searches are not always based on correct information about where the user doing the search actually is. If someone nearby can't find your business on a local search, this might be why.

Even better, Google Maps has become the de facto standard for computer users wanting map information. Google Maps, shown in Figure 1.1, makes it pretty easy to enter your default location for various searches. (The location is usually the address where the user actually is, but sometimes it's another address—someplace the user plans to be at in the future, for instance.) Not all users are savvy enough to use Google Maps properly for local searches, but more and more of them are.

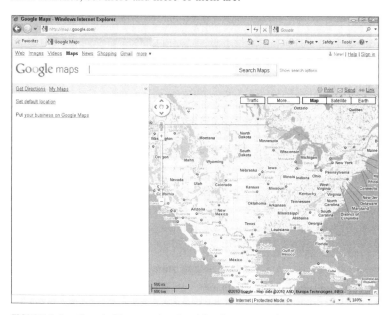

FIGURE 1.1   Google Maps makes local business searches easy.

TIP: **Get Places Savvy—and Show It**

Learn to use Google Maps for routine tasks such as finding nearby businesses and planning your trips. (This is what you'll want your customers to be doing.) If possible, get good enough at using Google Maps to be able to show customers in your store how to do it—with your own business as an example—so that they can use Google Maps themselves and teach others in turn. Your customers may well remember who taught them this important skill!

Getting Focused

Part of the initial thrill of the World Wide Web came from the fact that it was so darn, well, worldwide. It was easy to find any people and businesses who happened to have a web page, no matter where they were based, because so few people did.

However, as many web pages turned into robust websites, and as people started to depend on the Web for getting daily tasks done, the Web's very worldliness became a liability. You didn't need to know about florists in merry olde England if you were in New England, and vice versa.

Although geolocation services are making this better, they couldn't fix another problem. Small businesses tend to not have a website at all, or to have multipage websites, few of which are organized exactly like any other. A seemingly simple task such as finding the opening hours of the three florists nearest you remained difficult or even impossible.

What was needed, and what Google Places provides, is a single, more-or-less standardized web page with core information about a business, all in one place, and all available at one glance, or at worst by scrolling up and down—no clicking around.

The standard format also has to be easy for businesses to manage. In fact, Google Places is super easy; Google puts together a page about your business even if you don't do anything at all. That page, though, will be missing vital information that only you, as the business owner or manager, can reliably provide—which is where this book comes in.

NOTE: **Where Is Google Getting Its Information?**

Google Places has information for about 50 million places—but "only" about 4 million businesses and other organizations have claimed their Places page and, presumably, updated their information. Where does Google get the information to fill in the gaps? Google looks for information in various websites and directories, "scrapes" it from its original home, and puts it in your Google Places page. If some random website says that your wine shop is primarily in the beer business, or that you're only open on weekends, between sunset and dawn, you're stuck with that until you fix it!

Looking at a Google Places Page

A Google Places page should have all the key information about your business in one place. It does have an awful lot of what you need. Some of it is a bit buried, though.

It reminds me of a joke by the comedian Steve Martin about the famous martial arts movie *Crouching Tiger, Hidden Dragon*. He said he was disappointed not to see any tigers or dragons in the movie. That was, he realized, because "the tigers are crouching and the dragons are hidden."

Google Places pages are "crouching"; they aren't obvious, but they show up when you do certain things, as described in the next section. Some of the information in the reviews, such as ratings, is "hidden." You don't see it up front, where you expect it, and instead have to click a link to see it.

The Top of a Google Places Page

Let's take a look at a typical Google Places page and where the information comes from. Figure 1.2 shows the top part of a typical Places page that has not yet been claimed—that is, the owner has not yet added information and features to it.

Name, address, hours, category   Request for page to be claimed   Google Maps map
        Links to directions and reviews   Print | Email | Link area

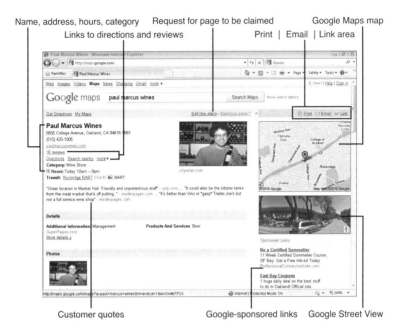

Customer quotes   Google-sponsored links   Google Street View

FIGURE 1.2   A Google Places page is a big calling card.

You can see that the page is unclaimed from the Edit This Place link and
the link next to it, Business Owner?, near the top of the window, just
above the picture of the founder. Google Places is essentially asking the
business owner to edit the page. After the page is claimed, the link will
appear as Owner-Verified Listing, and only the owner will be able to
update the information.

CAUTION: **Someone Can Pose as You**

Until you claim your Google Places listing, you, or anyone else, can
edit your business listing without verifying it. There are two problems here. The first is that anyone can put misinformation on the
Places page for your business, whether accidentally or on purpose.
The other is that visitors to your page don't see the link, **Owner-
Verified Listing**. Without the verification note, users may mistrust
the information—and perhaps mistrust your business as well.

NOTE: **Claimed or Unclaimed?**

The business listing shown here is for an unclaimed Google Pages business listing. The screen appears the same, though, for a claimed Google Pages listing if the user accessing the page is not currently logged in as the Google user whose account is tied to this business. See Lesson 3, "Using Google Places," for details.

The upper left of any page is where a user's eyes typically go first. That area of the Google Places page has crucial information for any potential customer:

- ▶ **Business Name:** This can be a tough one for some businesses, which might be known as "the bar on the corner" rather than "Albert's Drink-o-rama."

- ▶ **Address:** The address will help many people get to you; the Google Maps map on the right side should help many others.

- ▶ **Web Address:** Ironically, the Google Places page that gives so much crucial information might also get you more web traffic. Also, even a bad web address that's hard to guess or remember, or a site that would normally be tough to find through search, can be linked to from your Google Places page. See Lesson 11, "Advertising with Tags and AdWords," for details.

- ▶ **Category:** This was a problem for many businesses in the Yellow Pages days, but less of a problem online, with so many ways to search for a business besides by rigid categories. You still want to get the category right, though, to help searchers and to define who your competitors are.

▶ **Customer Quotes:** This area can be delightful or infuriating,
depending greatly on luck. For instance, in the quotes for Paul
Marcus Wines in Figure 1.2, you'll see a mention of some lobster
tanks in a shop next door that some poor wine shopper found
somewhat offensive! See Lesson 6, "Improving Your Google
Places Page," for more.

> TIP: **Click the Source of a Customer Quote**
>
> Click the source of a customer quote to find the full review that
> contains the quote and possibly other customer reviews on your
> business. You can't change the quotes that appear for your busi-
> ness, but a quote can be "bumped" as new reviews appear at vari-
> ous places around the Web.

▶ **Print | Email | Link Area:** This functionality makes it easy for
you or others to print out your Google Places page and hand it
around or to email it to others. The Link area displays a URL that
you can use to link to the page in a web page, email message,
instant message, or Twitter message.

▶ **Google Maps:** A strip down the right side on a web page is
called a *right-hand rail*, and information there often goes unseen.
The colorful, interactive Google Map should draw lots of attention and use, though.

▶ **Street View:** Street View is a great Google Maps feature, but
here the view is *from* the business, not *of* the business. Not the
best place to start. See Lesson 5, "Claiming Your Google Places
Page," for more information on Google Maps and its Street View
feature.

▶ **Sponsored Links:** These are ads relating to your area of business. The bad news is that they could easily distract restless web
surfers away from continuing on to get more information about,
or to visit, you. Lesson 11, "Advertising with Tags and
AdWords," tells you how you can create your own ads and distract people from other searches onto your site!

TIP: **Take Notes Now So That You Can Make Changes Later**
Check your Google Places page for your business, if there is one, and make a list of everything you like and don't like about it. Carefully put your thoughts into sections matching the sections on the Google Places page. Then, as you read this book, you can learn how to fix problems, as well as how to make your strong points even stronger.

"Below the Fold" on a Google Places Page

There are several areas of a Google Places page below the initial, core information. Depending on screen size, users unlikely to see these areas unless they scroll down. Such areas are called *below the fold* in web marketing jargon, and are considered much less valuable because so many users never bother to scroll down.

There are many major areas of a Google Places page that are often, or always, below the fold. Several of them are shown in Figure 1.3. They are as follows:

- ▶ **Details:** This information is copied, or *scraped*, from a site such as SuperPages.com. The entry shown in Figure 1.3 is, as the Brits would say, "a bit rubbish"; it describes Paul Marcus Wines as focused on beer!

- ▶ **Photos:** This is a huge area of opportunity for most businesses. Half a dozen or so well-chosen photos can be very attractive to customers. Paul Marcus Wines is lucky that, without trying, it has a photo of a very young Paul Marcus in the early days of his shop.

- ▶ **Reviews:** Many business owners live in fear of a bad review showing up on a site such as Yelp, Google Places, or other review sites. I've heard of a bartender being threatened with firing if he or she caused a second such bad review. See Lesson 6 for more.

- ▶ **Related Maps:** This area can be time-consuming, and it can have a lot of overlap among maps from a single source, but some users might explore it. It could bolster your business's credibility—or take users away to competitors.

Photos   Details   Google-sponsored links

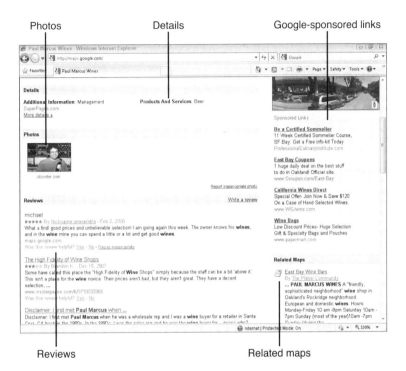

Reviews   Related maps

FIGURE 1.3   Important information lurks below the fold.

TIP: **Creating a Custom Related Map**

You can create your own Related Map that shows your business, but don't make it too "salesy." For instance, if you have a business that sells a particular, unusual product, you can create a Related Map of shops that sell that product. This is the kind of thing you should aim for—valuable information that happens to include your business, rather than hype that only benefits you. It's not guaranteed that Google will display a given map on your Google Places page, even if it prominently or repeatedly mentions your business.

> CAUTION: **Patience, Grasshopper**
>
> If you see inaccurate information in your Google Places page, it might be tempting to charge right in and start editing it. However, you should go through a step-by-step process to do this correctly, in a way that will work well for the future. See Lesson 3, "Using Google Places," for details.

There are three more areas below the fold, as shown in Figure 1.4. Along with reviews, they're among the most potentially contentious areas in Google Places:

▶ **Nearby Places You Might Like:** A range of sites, which includes sites also known as competitors! Google Places makes it very easy for your online visitors to consider going to another business similar to yours. Use this book to help you make such a strong online impression that most of them don't even consider it.

▶ **More About This Place:** These are websites that prominently mention your business. This is mostly good, but could say bad things about your business. It can lead to guilt by association if, for instance, a controversial site shows up in this section of your Google Places page, whether it recommends or disparages you.

▶ **User Content:** This is additional discussion of your business on the Web from sites that tend to attract a lot of comments. It can include YouTube videos, review articles, Wikipedia articles, and other resources. Again, this area is something you have little direct control over.

> NOTE: **Add More After You're Verified**
>
> After your listing is verified, you can add additional information, including photos (Lesson 10, "Posting Real-Time Updates"), videos (Lesson 8), coupons (Lesson 9, "Adding Coupons"), and real-time updates such as weekly specials (Lesson 13, "Using QR Codes and Getting Better Reviews"). See Lesson 5 for information on verifying your listing.

Nearby places you might like

More about this place

User Content

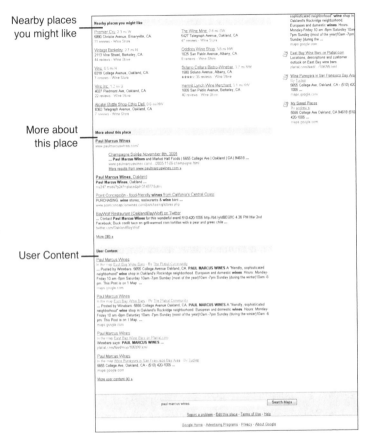

FIGURE 1.4   Nearby places can take away your customers.

Google Places, You, and the Competition

Your ultimate goal in improving your Google Places presence—and your other points of contact with customers, online and offline—is, to put it bluntly, to steal customers from your competitors. The ultimate goal of your competitors in improving their various kinds of contact is to steal business from you.

It used to be that many businesses had a certain amount of guaranteed business once they started up. If you were the only doctor, dentist, or vet in town, it was awfully hard for people to avoid you when they needed your kind of service. Same with a general store, a bank, or a drugstore.

However, with more people moving to cities, the widespread use of cars, and the stunning growth of online shopping, people have many options. If you stand out, there's much to gain. But if you fall behind, you can lose everything, as eager shoppers drive, bike, or even run past your shop, pick up their phone, or flood onto the Internet to buy from competitors.

Social media such as Twitter and Facebook, and geographically based services such as Foursquare, make such public mood swings even more dramatic. They strengthen the effect of a product, service, business, or location being seen as cool or not cool. You definitely want to be on the cool side!

A *carrotmob* is a group of people that has formed to "reward businesses who are making the most socially responsible decisions." The carrotmob will all flock to a chosen business on a given day, sending sales through the roof (see Figure 1.5). Doing a good job on marketing efforts such as Google Places can be the basis for helping you, not a competitor, to get carrotmobs and similar groups to come to your door.

The carrotmob, though, is just a dramatic example of something that's usually more gradual. Your potential customers make hundreds of little decisions that bring slightly more or slightly fewer people to your business, with a little more or a little less money ready to spend. Your Google Places presence is an important factor in influencing those decisions in your favor.

The Web has had, and is still having, a huge impact on locally based businesses. Local bookshops are the most dramatic example, closing by the thousands as online booksellers, led by Amazon.com, and super-sized bookstores (with the buying power to compete with online merchants) take over.

Web businesses have even changed the nature of the book business, creating devices such as the Kindle and the iPad that help people consume books electronically. Traditional booksellers are cut out of the loop entirely.

FIGURE 1.5   Carrotmobs reward socially responsible businesses.

Google Places is great because it gives you a way to get your voice heard online, and to help draw people to you based on the advantage given by your location. It can help you get business back, not only from local competition, but also from web-based competitors.

Having to maintain a Google Places presence might seem like a hassle sometimes—perhaps just another bunch of things to do, with complicated inputs and questionable outputs. It represents, though, a huge opportunity. The sooner you take advantage of it, the more you'll benefit.

TIP: **Know Thy Competition**

Find the Google Places pages for three locally based competitors. (They're probably listed in the Nearby Places You Might Like section of your own Google Places page, if you have one!) Compare the pluses and minuses of their Google Places page to your own to see where you might have an advantage already, and where you might want to improve your listing to win your fair share of business.

Summary

In this lesson, you learned about the basics of Google Places—what Google Places is for, what's on a typical Google Places page, and how you can use Google Places to stand out from all your competitors.

LESSON 2

Editing Your Google Places Pages

In this lesson, you'll learn where to find Google Places pages online and where to find help information and other resources, how people get to Google Places pages from a personal computer, and how they get to Google Places pages from a mobile phone. You'll then learn how to make initial edits to your Google Places page to correct any misinformation.

Where Is Google Places?

If you're going to be putting effort into making your Google Places page interesting and up-to-date, you probably need to know where Google Places pages exist and how people get to them. Then you can get the most out of your Google Places efforts. (And even find your own Google Places page online when you need to!)

Google Places is not, itself, a place. There's no website with the name Google Places where people go to search, on which you can find all the Google Places pages. Instead, Google generates Google Places pages and inserts them in its Google Search and Google Maps search results. Users also see Google Places pages through Google's voice directory, 1-800-GOOG-411, and Google Earth.

Google Places pages either show up directly, or are available in search results or via a link, in several instances:

▶ When someone directly searches on your business name or something close to it. The user must either include your town or city name in the search, be located in your local area, or doing a search specifically targeted to your local area (such as using the Search Nearby feature in Google Maps).

▶ When someone searches for your business category while including your town or city name in the search, while located in your local area, or while doing a search specifically targeted to your local area.

▶ When someone searches for terms related to your business while including your town or city name in the search, while located in your local area, or while doing a search specifically targeted to your local area.

To a certain extent, Google Places and localized Google search take the *world* out of the World Wide Web. They help users focus on their own current or desired location, getting results that are relevant to a relatively small geographic area.

If you've been using Google's tools for a while, you might be able to guess that the home of Google Places is http://places.google.com. However, when you go to that web address, you don't find a bunch of Google Places pages for various locations, businesses, and so on. You just find information for setting up your Google Places page. Google Places is like Gmail; when you visit the Google web page, you see information valid for your own account.

Google Places pages only show up in Google search results of various kinds. They don't have easy-to-remember URLs. For example, here's the URL leading you to the Google Places page for the Statue of Liberty in New York City, shown in Figure 2.1: http://maps.google.com/maps?f=q&source=s_q&gl=us&g=Grand+Canyon%2C+Uninc%2C+Arizona&q=statue+of+liberty&btnG=Search+Maps.

The point is that Google Places pages don't exist anywhere particular. They're partly pregenerated by Google and partly assembled at the time that users search for a particular place. They come into existence when needed, and then disappear again until the next relevant search.

This is really good for users because they get fresh, up-to-date information. However, it's tough on owners and managers of businesses and other kinds of places. You no doubt value continuity and predictability; Google's constant updating and resulting unpredictability make Google Places hard to, well, manage (which is what owners and managers do).

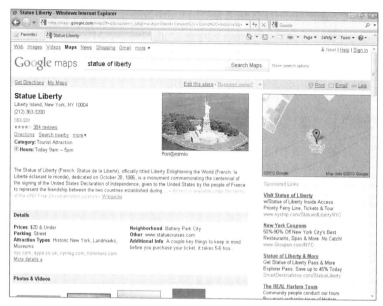

FIGURE 2.1   Use Google Places to learn how to visit Lady Liberty.

Your job in using Google Places is not made any easier by the fact that information about how to use Google Places is scattered all over various websites. Here are the key sites maintained by Google itself:

▶ **Google Places:** http://places.google.com—the home page for Google Places.

▶ **Google Places Support:** http://google.com/support/places—go here to get your questions about Google Places answered.

▶ **Google Places Videos:** http://www.youtube.com/googleplaces—YouTube-based instruction videos about how to use Google Places.

▶ **Lat Long Blog:** http://google-latlong.blogspot.com—the official blog for Google Maps, including Google Places.

▶ **Business Photos:** http://maps.google.com/help/maps/businessphotos/—where to go for information about getting Google to take photos of your business. See Lesson 7, "Adding Photos," for more information.

▶ **Google Favorite Places:** http://www.google.com/help/maps/
   favoriteplaces/business/index.html—sign up to be considered as a
   Favorite Place, and learn about QR codes, both described in
   Lesson 10, "Posting Real-Time Updates."

Getting to Google Places Pages

It's possible to be a regular user of Google Places pages and not even
know it. A Places page isn't labeled as such when you use it. The page is
labeled either Google Places or Google Search. The word *place* does
appear, but in a low-key way.

CAUTION: **Explaining Google Places to Others Is Tricky**
When telling customers, friends, and others about using Google
Places, they'll probably be confused—they don't see the words
Google Places featured in their regular use of the Web. Be ready to
explain or, preferably, show them your Google Places presence, and
how to access it anytime they want.

Many people who use Google Places probably don't even think much
about how they get to the page. It just looks like helpful information
assembled by Google.

There are six main ways that a user will get to your Google Places page
(or to a competitor's), as follows:

▶ Through Google Search on a personal computer

▶ Through Google Search on a mobile phone

▶ Through a Google Maps search on a personal computer

▶ Through a Google Maps search on a mobile phone

▶ Through Quick Reference (QR) codes (as covered in Lesson 10)

▶ Through competitor listings at the bottom of a Places page(!), as
   described in Lesson 1, "Introducing Google Places"

For our purposes here, I'm using the term *personal computer* for a laptop or desktop Windows PC or Macintosh with a typical laptop widescreen (13") or bigger. A mobile phone will typically have a 4" screen.

The difference between using a personal computer or a mobile device is important. When someone is using a personal computer, she sees a lot of information at once. (For instance, I'm writing this on an HP laptop with a second monitor attached to it, just so that I can work on and see more "stuff" at once.) You can assume that the user has a bit of time.

Even on a personal computer, people will often scan quickly and make snap judgments. But they can see a lot of data, and do a lot of exploring and comparing if they want. They'll tend to do this when deciding on something important, such as where to buy jewelry or where to go on a date.

When people are using a mobile device, you can assume they are on the go—walking or, heaven forbid, driving or bicycling while using their mobile. They can see only a small amount of screen space and are going to lack interest in comparing a lot of alternatives. They want the right answer from the little-bitty screen in front of them, now.

You have to think of this as you prioritize your efforts to get your Google Places page right. What's really going to grab someone on each platform? On Google Search results, where there may be other ways to get the same information, versus Google Maps, where the Google Places page might be more likely to be used?

Tablet computers such as the iPad are different still. Figure 2.2 shows an example of Google Street View, a feature prominently offered on many Google Places pages, on the iPad.

People love tablet computers because they feel so personal—much more so, paradoxically, than a "personal computer." The screen is somewhere between a super-big mobile phone screen and a small personal computer screen. They tend to allow only one main task to be actively happening at a time, either because the system is built that way or because the limited screen space allows the user to really manage only one active window at a time.

The way tablets are used, though, tend to fall into a personal computer-like situation, where the user is at home with his feet up and has time to search around, and a mobile phone-type situation, where the user is on the move—we all hope, not driving—and is in a big hurry to get one or two key facts. So, you don't really need to think of tablets specifically when you're planning your efforts on your Google Places page.

FIGURE 2.2   Google Street View looks fantastic on the iPad.

Google Search and Google Places

The most obvious place to want your Google Places page to appear is on a Google Search page. Businesses spend millions of dollars a year on search engine optimization, known by its initials as SEO.

All these businesses want to come in at or near the top of Google search results for keywords relevant to their business. For instance, a business specializing in political T-shirts might try hard to "own" the names of well-known politicians, as well as the names of politicians who might become well known in the future. Such a business, where search is tied directly to an impulse purchase, could be a big customer for SEO.

> **NOTE: Linked-To Sites Get Better Search Results Placement**
>
> Google Search gives better search results placement to pages that have a lot of frequently used pages pointing to them. If everyone who mentions starfish on the Web links to the Wikipedia entry for starfish, that Wikipedia page is going to get high search results placement indeed. So, when you claim and use your Google Places page, along with your website, and use each of them to point to the other, you get better Google Search results for both pages. Then, the more links you get to your website or your Google Places page, the better the Google Search results for both.

Your Google Places page is like a shortcut to higher search engine rankings. Google tends to put Places pages high up in its search results. Links back and forth between your Places page and your website also tend to boost the rankings for both pages.

Figure 2.3 shows how Google web search results look for the phrase *wine shop* for a search done from Oakland, California. There are a few things worth noting:

▶ **Wrong location:** Google thinks I'm searching from Santa Rosa. That's because my Google Voice phone number, which I picked to be easy to remember, happens to be a Santa Rosa-based number. I could easily correct this, but many of your potential customers won't. Location errors are common for Google Search searches.

▶ **Main focus on web URLs:** Notice that all the web addresses—technically called uniform resource locators, or URLs—shown directly in search results are for websites of various companies, not Google Places pages. Companies work so hard for good Google search results for their websites that they would be very upset if Google directly pushed Google Places sites instead.

▶ **High placement for Google Maps and Google Places pages:** Note that the Google Maps map with business results shows above the fold. Clicking on this map, as you'll see in the section on Google Maps later in this lesson, puts the user just a click away from a bunch of Google Places results.

FIGURE 2.3   Google Search results bring Google Places pages into reach.

Users can also go directly to a Google Places page by clicking the number of reviews (such as **37 reviews**). This link takes them to the top of the Google Places page, from which they have to click on a link or scroll down to see the actual reviews. So, there are no Google Places URLs visible on the page, but Google Places pages are still prominent in the results.

Now let's look at results for the same search on a mobile phone—in this case, coincidentally, a Google Nexus One phone, powered by Google's Android operating system for phones. (Android is used in Motorola's Droid line of phones, and many other phones and devices.) Google Search is also prominently available on the iPhone, the other major line of app phones, as well as Android-powered phones.

Figure 2.4 shows the search results. (The screen seems close to being personal computer-sized only because it's reduced very little, whereas the personal computer screen shots are reduced quite a bit.) Note that the location is in Oakland, as it should be—my mobile phone uses its GPS location or

Wi-Fi signal, not the phone number, to determine where it is. Mobile users will almost always have accurate location data as a basis for their searches.

FIGURE 2.4 Mobile web search shows Google Maps and Google Places links.

Note the far smaller amount of information on the mobile phone screen.

There's only one normal, or organic, search result—then the Google Maps result, still above the fold. You'd almost think that Google was giving the very top positions to organic search, while still making sure that Google Maps and Google Places always make it above the fold.

Paul Marcus Wines, the nearby wine shop whose Google Places page was shown in Lesson 1, is just below the fold, visible after scrolling down just a little bit.

> TIP: **Get Your Listing Shown in Search Results**
>
> Google shows just a few businesses next to the map that appears in search results—seven businesses for some searches, three for others, and just one for searches on a mobile phone. See Lesson 15, "Improving Search Engine Results," for tips on getting your listing into these highly visible results.

For mobile search, web URLs are not shown, and the business links go straight to Google Places pages! Although businesses are rightly worried about their personal computer search results, Google is making sure that its own offerings place quite high on the fast-growing mobile web.

> NOTE: **No Google Maps Presence on the iPad...Yet**
>
> I tried the same search on an iPad as on a Windows PC, and there was no Google Maps presence on the first page of search results, and therefore no Google Places links. This could change in the future, and could also be different on other tablet computers.

Google Maps Search and Google Places

Google Maps is an amazing tool, and is getting more and more use. It's already become the default online tool for geographically based searches on personal computers and mobile phones, displacing many competitors around the world.

Let's quickly look at the search results for a Google Maps search. Note that, if the user half knows what she's doing, the location searched will always be the area she intends to search.

> TIP: **Search Results Depend on Where You Start the Search**
>
> The local search results that a Google Maps user gets depends on where he sets the default location to, or where he starts from when using the Search Nearby feature. Most users are on top of this, but some are just confused and search in locations they don't intend to.

Figure 2.5 shows the results for a local search on the term *wine shop*, after clicking one of the results. Five shops show up in an area roughly a mile and a half square around where I live. One of them—result B, the third result from the top—is our friends at Paul Marcus Wines.

FIGURE 2.5   Google Maps search for *wine shop*.

The results aren't perfect. The first result, McCrum Oliver Wines, is a distributor—not of that much interest to your typical shopper. The rest, though, are pretty good. (The fourth result, Rockridge Market Hall, is a specialty grocery store, next to Paul Marcus Wines, that carries a few wines along with a lot of gourmet food, condiments, and so on.) Scrolling down, the next four results are all specialty shops mostly or entirely devoted to wine.

Overall, the results for the term *wine shop* in the Google Maps-based search are much better than for the same search in Google Search.

After you get a strong Google Places presence, consider encouraging—even showing—your customers how to use Google Places to find you, and featuring this information prominently on your website. You want customers to always be looking for local shops with the products they need, and to consider your shop their best bet for service and selection.

The Google Maps search results for *wine shop* on mobile search are quite different, as shown in Figure 2.6. An ad shows up at the top, and results with lots of reviews show up first, even when they're farther away. Our friends at Paul Marcus Wines are in an unlucky 13th place, several pages of scrolling down, and beneath another ad.

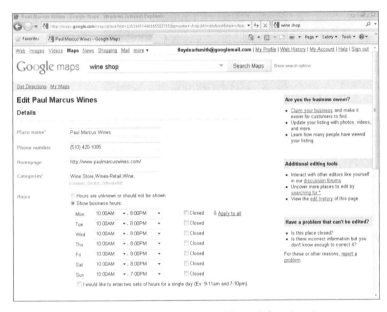

FIGURE 2.6   Google Maps search using mobile web for *wine shop*.

It looks like Google is, well, favoring what it calls Favorite Places—businesses with lots of online recognition, online traffic, and reviews. Read more about Favorite Places, and how to try to become one or keep your status as one, in Lesson 14, "Improving Search Engine Results."

Editing Your Google Places Page

Even before you verify ownership of your Google Places page (see Lesson 5, "Claiming Your Google Places Page"), you can make certain changes to the page's information:

▶ **Place name:** The name of your business. Make sure this matches your telephone directory listing, Yellow Pages listing, other marketing and advertising, and so forth.

▶ **Phone number:** This is a hugely important means of moving someone from web surfing to buying from you. If you're using a mobile phone rather than a land line, make sure your number is a local area code—and even a local exchange (the first three digits of the seven-digit local number should be the same as other local phone numbers) to reassure people that you're real.

▶ **Home page:** Your website, if you have one. This is an important complement to your Google Places page.

▶ **Categories:**The categories, similar to Yellow Pages categories, that your business goes in. See Appendix A, "Places Categories," for details.

▶ **Hours:** Knowing your open hours is hugely important to customers. Google does not provide a clear way to indicate holiday hours. I recommend that you use real-time updates to indicate holiday hours, as described in Lesson 14.

▶ **Address:** This needs to be right, of course, or you'll lose business.

▶ **Location of the business entrance:** Google lets you specify this quite precisely in Google Maps. Check and, if needed, fix this carefully—you don't want to be sending valued customers to the wrong door!

TIP: **Make Voice Messages and Places Business Hours Consistent**

Put your business's hours of operation and website address on your phone voice message as well as on your Google Places page. Update your phone voice message around holiday times to indicate your holiday hours, too. There's not much that's more irritating than calling a business, not getting an answer, and not knowing when you will.

Anyone can make these changes—which might seem alarming. Google is hoping for two things to occur: first, that business owners will claim their listings, as described in Lesson 5, carrying most of the load; second, that interested people will take on the job of keeping information up-to-date for listings not claimed by a business owner.

This approach to gathering information is called *crowdsourcing* and is quite powerful. The highly ranked popular site, Wikipedia, is crowdsourced, as are the reviews on Amazon.com and, indeed, on Google Places pages.

However good crowdsourcing is, it's clear that no one has a greater interest in having accurate information on your Google Places page than you do. So, you should take on the job of maintaining your information on Google Places yourself by editing your Google Places page right away—as described here—and then by claiming and improving your listing, as described in Lesson 5.

TIP: **Make Edits and Then Verify the Ownership**

You—or anyone—can make certain edits to your Google Places page, as described here. Make these changes right away to fix any mistakes. Then, as soon as you can, claim your page by verifying ownership, as described in Lesson 5. Verifying ownership locks out others from making changes and enables you to add photos, videos, coupons, and more.

Follow these steps to edit your Google Places page before verifying the connection to your business, as described in Lesson 5:

1. Open Google Maps in your browser at http://maps.google.com.

2. Sign in to your Google account. If you don't have a Google account, sign up for one as described in Lesson 4, "Signing Up for a Google Account."

   When editing your Google Places page before the link to your business has been verified, it doesn't matter what Google account you sign in to. After you've verified the link, as described in Lesson 5, only the account that you used for verification will work for editing your Google Places page.

3. To find your business, enter the business name and town or city name in the Google Maps search area, and then click the **Search Maps** button. Your business might appear in the list of search results.

4. If your business does not appear, try variations on the name and town or city name. Also enter a nearby address, or pan and zoom on the map to center it on your business location, and then click the actual address to see whether your business is listed there. If you find it, go to step 3. If you do not, go to Lesson 5.

5. In the entry for your business, click the **More Info** link. The Google Places page appears.

6. Click the **Edit This Place** link. The Edit page for your business appears. The Edit page for Paul Marcus Wines is shown in Figure 2.7.

7. Make changes to your business information as needed: place name, phone number, website home page, description, categories, hours, address, and location of the entrance.

   For categories, enter up to five categories that are appropriate for your business. You can enter category names as they come to mind. As you type, Google uses your partial entry to display suggestions in a scrolling list. You can also enter a custom category

FIGURE 2.7 You can make basic edits to your Places page before verifying it.

name or use the list in Appendix A to use the category names suggested by Google. See Appendix A for a complete discussion.

The description is important marketing copy, but it should be written simply, and from the perspective of an independent observer, not a business owner. The description text can also help with search engine optimization for your business; see Lesson 14 for details.

For the location of the entrance, use Google Maps to move the location of the indicator around until it aligns with the entrance you want customers to use. You can zoom in and out, pan, and switch among Map, Satellite, and Hybrid Views.

8. When you've finished making changes, click the **Publish** button. Your information will be published to the Web. The changes might take anywhere from a few minutes to a few hours to appear.

Summary

In this lesson, you learned where to find Google Places pages, help information and other resources, and how people get to Google Places pages from a personal computer or a mobile phone. You then learned how to make initial edits to your Google Places page.

Using Google Places

In this lesson, you'll learn how to take the customer's point of view to your Google Places page and how a business website relates to it. You'll also learn how customers use reviews, as well as directions, Street View, service areas, and other features related to Google Maps.

Taking the Customer's Point of View

One of the biggest problems in putting information online is that you start thinking like a publisher—trying to get information right, but perhaps not knowing how. The trick is to think like a user: Identify with what users want and try to give it to them.

First of all, your overall goal is to get people to buy from you. In most cases, this means getting the user to do a mode switch—to stop using the Web and actually come visit you in person. The job of your Google Places page is to get users to want to visit you, and then to actually help them do it.

With that in mind, let's look closely at a Google Places page and see what a user can actually do with it.

Here are some of the questions that users might have in mind when they visit your Google Places page:

▶ **What is this page?** Google Places pages aren't labeled as such, and there's no About This Page information on the page itself. My suggestion here is that you provide information about your Google Places page on your website, if you have one.

▶ **Is there detailed information about the business?** The user will want to know your address, your hours of operation, how to get there, what you sell (your business category as well as specific products and services), prices, and your phone number (to follow up). The most important information here might be your phone number—users can call you, confirm what they want to know, and then decide whether to visit.

Most of the detailed information that customers are likely to want is part of your Google Places listing, as shown in Figure 3.1. You just have to make sure it's all accurate and up-to-date. (The Google Places screen shown in Figure 3.1 shows the Search Nearby area open, as will be explained in the "Getting Directions" section, later in this lesson.) As for the specific products, services, and prices, you can provide some or all of this on your website—while also encouraging people to call.

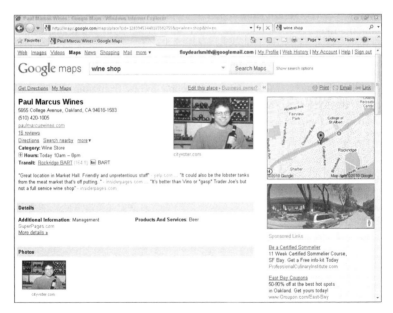

FIGURE 3.1   Google Pages puts contact information and reviews front and center.

▶ **What do other people think?** Do other people like your customer service, products, services, and prices? This is captured in reviews, related maps, web links, and so on. For the brief quotes listed just under the Hours area near the top, you can click a link from the quote's source to see the full quote and possibly other reviews of your business from the same site.

▶ **What about the competition?** People used to see competitors in the Yellow Pages; now they see them through Google Places section called Nearby Places You Might Like. If this drives you a bit nuts, rest assured that it might bring you business (from other people's Google Places pages), as well as take some away.

This brief overview should give you some idea of why Google Places exists and why it's structured the way it is. Google wants to put all the information the customer wants on one large calling card. The better job it does—and the more it does to get you to bulk up your own Google Places page—the more people use Google Search (see Lesson 14, "Improving Search Engine Results") and Google Maps (see Lesson 3, "Using Google Places"), AdWords (see Lesson 11, "Advertising with Tags and AdWords"), and all the rest.

TIP: **Eat Your Own Dog Food with Google Places**

When you use your own product, or one you recommend, technology and marketing people call it "eating your own dog food." Because you want others to use Google Places to find your business, try using Google Places for your own shopping and other chores. You'll quickly develop a feel for improvements you can make to the Google Places presence for your own business.

The Role of the Website

Google Places fills part of the role of a website (see Lesson 14), for those users who go to Google Places first. Google Places provides most of or all the contact information that experts are always saying should be prominent on any website.

For these users, your website—if you have one—is complementary, providing additional information and detail. Your website should also give more of a feel for your business's personality, but not all local business websites are well designed enough to do that.

> TIP: **Simpler Websites Often Look Better on Phone Screens**
>
> A relatively unstructured website like the Paul Marcus Wines site shown in Figures 3.1 and 3.2 might display better on a mobile phone web browser than a more highly structured site that looks more polished on a personal computer screen.

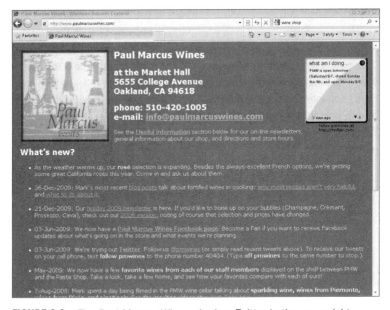

FIGURE 3.2   The Paul Marcus Wines site has Twitter in the upper-right corner of the web page.

Figure 3.2 shows the web page for Paul Marcus Wines, the Oakland wine shop whose Google Places page is shown in the first three figures in Lesson 1, "Introducing Google Places." You can see that, graphically, it's very simple. Note, though, how prominent contact information is and how Twitter is integrated into the site.

Figure 3.3 shows the bottom half of the same web page. Although there aren't explicit navigation tabs on the site—big buttons reading Contact Us, About Us, and so on—the site does have some depth, with links to a bunch of online Paul Marcus newsletters.

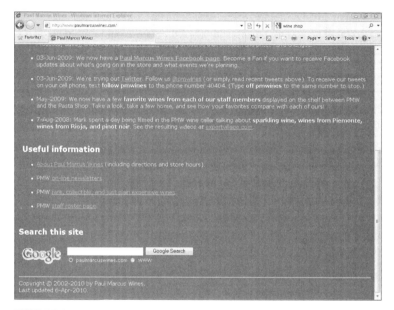

FIGURE 3.3   The Paul Marcus Wines site has links to newsletters in the lower-left corner of the page.

> NOTE: **Wine Site Updated**
>
> The Paul Marcus Wine site has been updated since the screen shots in Figures 3.1, 3.2, and 3.3 were taken. Visit http://www.paulmarcuswines.com to see the latest.

Using Reviews

Customers love reviews. Or perhaps it's more accurate to say that *potential* customers love reviews because bad reviews will keep them away.

The advent of online reviews has been a real shock to some local businesses. Business owners were used to assuming that people would just expect their business to be competent—and that, in today's atomized world, any bad news might not get around too fast.

So, online reviews can cause a great deal of pain for business owners, managers, and staff. I know a bartender who was threatened with being fired after a bad customer review with her name on it appeared on Yelp.com. She was told that one more of the same would lead to her getting her walking papers.

Similar conversations are likely occurring all over the place as Google Places follows Yelp as a prominent resource for online reviews. Some of the reviews come from Yelp, and others are gathered from other sites. Users can also post reviews directly to your Google Places page.

Google Search and Google Maps search puts the number of reviews prominently on search results pages and on the top of the Google Places page. To see the actual reviews, though, the user has to click a link at the top of the page or scroll down the page. (People don't like to make extra efforts online; research shows that having to click a link or scroll means that many users will never see information such as your Google Places reviews.)

You should encourage good reviews, first by giving excellent customer service, and then by explicitly encouraging customers to put their opinions—hopefully, good ones—online. See Lesson 9, "Adding Coupons," for details.

Getting Directions

One of the toughest problems for local businesses is giving directions to customers—or, again, potential customers. People call from all over and have vastly different needs in terms of where they're coming from, how specific the directions need to be, what landmarks they're familiar with, and so forth.

Google solves this problem for many millions of people. Google Maps has become the world's most-used online mapping and directions software. Google Maps results are integrated in many searches carried out on Google Search. Many users also use Google Maps directly for looking for local businesses, getting directions, and so on.

Google Maps is also found on popular smartphones, including the two market leaders, the iPhone and Android phones. On many Android phones, Google Maps offers free turn-by-turn navigation for car drivers and others. This helps the smartphone to replace a GPS navigation device that can cost hundreds of dollars.

So, the directions link and maps shown on Google Places is very important for helping you get business. On a Google Places page such as the one shown in Figure 3.1, there are actually four different directions-related links above the fold—that is, visible on the first screen of results:

> ▶ **Directions:** Clicking the Directions link brings up a Google Maps screen with the destination set to the business location featured in the Google Places listing, as shown in Figure 3.4. Depending on the location you're in, the options for directions might include driving, public transportation, walking, biking, and more.

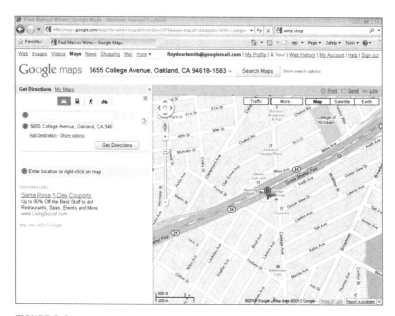

FIGURE 3.4   Directions help your customers reach you—literally.

> ▶ **Search Nearby:** Clicking the **Search Nearby** link causes a small box to open beneath the link (as shown in Figure 3.1), enabling

the user to enter a search term, such as *bookstores*. Google Maps then opens to show the area around the business shown in Google Places, with destinations fitting the search term shown.

▶ **Map:** Google Places shows a small version of a Google Map. Clicking it opens up Google Maps with the display centered on the business shown in Google Places.

▶ **Street View:** Google Places shows a small version of Street View for the area around the business, where available. Street View photos are gathered, and stitched together, by specially equipped cars and trucks sent out by Google. Clicking the **Street View** image causes Google Maps to open up with a larger version of the Street View image shown. From there, the user can pan, zoom, move around, return to a normal Map View, and so on.

If you aren't familiar with Google Maps, experiment with all of these features. Try searching for a type of business, for instance, and then clicking the + and − buttons on the map screen to make the map zoom in and out. You'll see the list of businesses changing to the ones that fit on the screen after zooming. The effect is confusing, but sensible when you think about it.

Use Google Maps in your own daily life so that you become quite comfortable with it. You might find yourself giving a guided tour of Google Maps over the phone to a confused customer who's trying to visit your business!

CAUTION: **Google Doesn't Always Get the Picture**

Google doesn't check the details of Google Places pages manually, and one place this can show up is in Street View. Many times, the Street View image is shown on your Google Places page. And when Google Maps opens onto Street View after the user clicks the image, she is not looking at your business—which, of course, is what you would want—but somewhere nearby.

Seeing Service Areas

Google Maps has a relatively new feature called *service areas*. This feature shows a colored area on the map to indicate where a given business offers service.

Plumbers, pizza parlors, and pet shampooers are among the businesses that might want to specify a service area. The service area tells users whether they can expect a given business to serve the address where they live or work.

Displaying the service area is optional. On the bubble that gives basic information about a business, the option Show Service Area appears. If the user clicks the link, the service area appears. Also, the option changes to Hide Service Area.

Users might not see service areas because they don't click the link—or they might see them but ignore them, hoping to get served even if they're outside of the specified area. Still, as more businesses use, and depend on, service areas, users will get more accustomed to seeing that they're present, displaying them, and depending on them to choose where to seek products and services.

Summary

In this lesson, you learned how to take the customer's point of view to your Google Places page and how a business website relates to it. You also learned how customers use reviews as well as directions, Street View, service areas, and other features related to Google Maps.

LESSON 4

Signing Up for a Google Account

In this lesson, you'll set up a Google account for your business. (You need one to claim, or create, your Google Places page.) The recommended way to do this is by creating a Gmail account. You'll choose your Gmail login name—almost as important a task as choosing a domain name for your website—and learn about other Google services that can help your business grow.

How to Get a Google Account for Your Business

You need a Google account to manage your Google Places page. I have some very specific recommendations about how to manage this:

▶ Create a business Google account:Create a Google account specifically for your business, in addition to any individual accounts you or others involved with the business may have. Why? Your Google Places page is an asset of the business, not of any one employee or even the boss. It should be managed as an asset. For instance, a new owner would want to inherit the Google account and change the password at a certain point.

TIP: **Use a Business-Specific Google Account**

Google recommends creating and using a business-specific account, which can be shared by multiple users, for editing your business information (not an individual's account). See Lesson 6, "Improving Your Google Places Page," for details.

▶ **Use Gmail for your business:** Use Gmail within the business account to manage some of or all your business-related email. Gmail has very powerful mail-importing and -forwarding capabilities, plus very large storage capacity (many gigabytes and growing), making it a great traffic cop and repository for managing your business email among various business and personal email accounts, even if not all of them are Gmail accounts.

▶ **Create your business Google account via Gmail:** You can use any email account to create a Google account, but creating a business-specific Gmail account is the easiest and most consistent way to do it.

▶ **Use a business-friendly name:** Use a business-friendly name for your business account and Gmail. It used to be considered the height of fashion to have a specific domain name for your business, such as paulmarcuswines.com, and to have all employees use email names within the domain, such as marktheman@paulmarcuswines.com. Now it's considered quite acceptable to use Gmail for similar purposes, with a Gmail address such as paulmarcuswines@gmail.com. (You can have both, of course.)

▶ **Use related services for your business account:** Use Google services such as Google Calendar, Google Groups, Picasa for photo storage, Blogger for blogging, YouTube, Google Voice for phone management, and Google Docs. Figure 4.1 shows a page full of Google services.

Google's services match up well against the competition on a one-for-one basis, and as a group they offer power and ease of use that you can't get any other way, especially at no cost—in most cases.

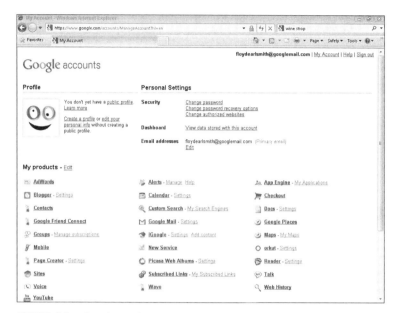

FIGURE 4.1   Google services can power your whole business.

> NOTE: **Use Your Freedom of Choice in Email Addresses**
>
> It's very slick and professional to have an email address on your Google Places page that matches the domain name of your company's website. However, it's not necessary these days for smaller businesses, at least, because people have become accustomed to the use of Gmail accounts for business. If you do use an email account with your company's domain name, you can direct that email account to automatically forward its email to the Google email account you create or just work directly from the email account that matches your domain name.

▶ **Consider moving staffers to Google services:** It's really confusing for different people who are part of the business to be using different tools, so consider asking, or even requiring, staffers to move partly or completely to Google services for work purposes.

▶ **Consider using Google Apps:** Google Apps is a paid service ($50 per user per year) that includes much more Gmail storage, the option to turn off text ads in Gmail, Google Docs storage, better security, improved customer support, and an uptime guarantee.

TIP: **Consider Moving to Gmail**

You can use a non-Gmail email account to create a Google account. If you already use a business-specific Yahoo! account, for instance, you can use that. However, Yahoo! mail and other non-Google mail programs have limitations that you might want to move away from. Consider starting over with a Gmail account; you can use Gmail to automatically import email from the old account, and even to send out email so that it appears to come from that same account, even though it's actually all handled in Gmail.

Choosing Your Gmail Login Name

When you create your Gmail account, or any Google account, you'll need to create a login name that is unique—not already in use by someone else. There are probably already a few Top Hat Liquor stores in the world, so the email address tophatliquor@gmail.com is probably already taken. Consider various options before you try to sign up to your account. Possibilities include the following:

▶ **The straight business name:** This is simply putting the words in the business name together, as in tophatliquor@gmail.com. This is the easiest for customers, suppliers, and others to remember.

▶ **An abbreviated version of the business name:** You can use a shortened version of the name, such as thliquor@gmail.com, if that's available. The full name is more memorable, but if it's too long, an abbreviated version might be better.

▶ **Adding the locality to the business name:** You can add the area, town, or city you're in to your business name to make a login name. Try not to add length. This is easy in a city like San Francisco (*sf* for short) and hard in Oakland or Seattle. You might have to use an abbreviated version of the business name with the locality to make the whole thing digestible.

For Paul Marcus Wines in Oakland, the ideal name is paulmarcuswines@gmail.com. If that were taken, using the locality and an abbreviated version of the business name would yield pmwinesrockridge@gmail.com.

Another possibility would be paulmarcuswinesrr@gmail.com, but many people might think the *rr* stood for *railroad*.

The signup process lets you get started and then asks you for the login name you want to use. Unfortunately, it's easy to start the process, find your first choice is gone, and maybe your second, and then enter something in haste that you regret later. Either brainstorm possible names before starting or be ready to break off the signup process if your first choice or two aren't available. Take the time to come up with a name you can live with in the long run.

If you really get stuck, you can use an existing non-Gmail business email account, or even create such an account with the username—but not the email host—that you want. Use a Gmail account if possible.

CAUTION: **Be Specific, Not Generic**

Avoid generic names such as oaklandwine@gmail.com. Your business doesn't really handle all the wine sold in Oakland. Also avoid cute names, especially controversial ones, such as drinkupoakland@gmail.com. People know your business by two (hopefully) non-controversial facts: its name and location. Try to stick to these known quantities when coming up with your business email name.

Signing Up for Your Gmail Account

Follow these steps to set up a Gmail account, which is the easiest and most powerful way to create a Google account:

1. Go to the Gmail home page at http://www.gmail.com.

If you are not already signed in to a Gmail account, the Welcome to Gmail page appears. If you are already signed in to a Google account, your user identifier appears in the upper-right corner of the web page, along with a Sign Out link. If the Google account you are logged in to includes the use of Gmail, your Gmail inbox will appear.

2. If you are already signed into a Google account, click the **Sign Out** link.

The Gmail home page appears.

3. Click the **Create an Account** button.

The Create a Google Account – Gmail page appears, as shown in Figure 4.2.

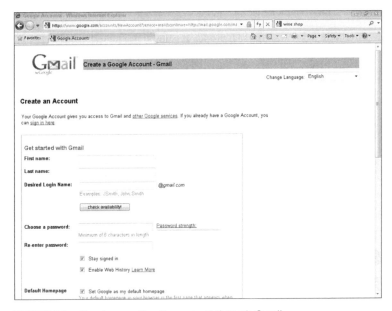

FIGURE 4.2   Create your Google account through Gmail.

4. Enter your first and last name.

You can use your personal name—you can always change this later—or a generic name, such as Store Manager.

5. Enter your desired login name, and then click the **Check Availability** button. Keep trying until you find a name that's suitable for your business and available.

This can be tricky because you can't use a name that's already in use as a Google account name. Use a name that's as close to your business name as possible. If the name you want is chosen, consider adding your town or city name—and shortening the other parts of the name if needed. See the previous section for details.

If you can't find a name you like a lot right off the bat, stop the process, consider alternatives, and discuss your options with people you trust. If you really get stuck, you can use a non-Gmail email address to create your Google account. In that case, start the preceding process at http://www.google.com, not http://www.gmail.com, and skip the login name step.

6. Choose a password.

   Keep your password stored someplace safe because it's an important asset of your business, and change it periodically, including whenever an employee who might have known the password leaves the business.

7. Enter the remaining fields.

   Be sure to enter a recovery email address as a backup—but be aware that anyone currently involved in the business could move on, including you, so don't count on it too much.

8. Review the terms of service, and then click the **I Accept Create My Account** button.

   Your account is created.

TIP: **Check Out Your Account Name**

After you set up your account, ask around and make sure that the account name you chose is a good one. If it's not, create a new account with the name you want, and then delete the old one. (To do this, sign in at the http://www.google.com/accounts/login page. Next to the My Products list, click the **Edit** link, and from there you can delete your account.)

You can use your Gmail account for a wide variety of purposes—more than just about any other kind of email account. You can use your Gmail account to retrieve email from your other accounts, to send email in the guise of other accounts, and more.

Your Gmail account is very powerful and flexible. To get the most out of it, ask a friend or colleague who has experience with Gmail or find a book. Also, sign in to Gmail and click the **Help** link to learn more.

Using Google Services

After you have your Google account, you can use all sorts of Google services.

This book already prominently mentions Google Places, Google Maps, and Gmail. Here are brief descriptions of a dozen or so other top services, in addition to Gmail—some of which you just about need to get the most out of Google Places:

▶ **AdWords:** AdWords (see Lesson 11, "Advertising with Tags and AdWords") enables you to place small text ads for your business alongside the unbiased, organic search results that Google is famous for. AdWords is a great complement to Google Places and to your website.

▶ **Analytics:** Your Google Dashboard (see Lesson 14, "Improving Search Engine Results") gives basic statistics for visits to your Google Places page. Google Analytics takes analysis a big step further for your website. Analytics is intense, but worthwhile if you really want to get the most out of your site.

▶ **Blogger:** This is an easy-to-use blogging tool, perhaps the easiest one to start out with. Having a blog, a website, and a Google Places page for your business, all linking to each other as much as reasonably possible, helps raise search results for all three.

▶ **Calendar:** Google Calendar is a shared online calendar that you can access from anywhere that you have a web connection, including from a smartphone. Calendar makes it easy to get to appointments, manage employee schedules, arrange for deliveries, and so on.

▶ **Checkout:** Google Checkout is an easy way to take payments on your website. It isn't wildly popular, but seems reliable enough.

▶ **Contacts:** A powerful way to manage contacts online—although, as with any such software, managing contacts properly takes time.

▶ **Docs:** Google Docs, shown in Figure 4.3, gives you online word processing, spreadsheets, and presentations. The files are stored online, so you don't have to be at work to access them, and they can even be edited by two or more people at once.

FIGURE 4.3   Not only is Google Docs free, you can share work "live."

▶ **Groups:** Google Groups enables you to set up email subscription lists, share files easily, and much more.

▶ **Picasa:** You're going to need photos and videos for your Google Places page, and perhaps your website as well. Google's Picasa online photo management service has the best integration with other Google services, and an accompanying personal computer software package, too.

▶ **Sites:** Sites is for creating simple websites, and has features that make it very useful indeed for intranets and extranets—websites that aren't available to the public, but to only a trusted few insiders.

▶ **Talk:** Google Talk supports instant messaging among users on computers and smartphones, enabling you to keep in touch whenever you want to. Google Talk is very well integrated with Gmail.

▶ **Voice:** Google Voice enables you to have a flexible, virtual number, which you can assign to several phones, and then switch among them as needed. Very good for small business.

▶ **YouTube:** Both Picasa (see the Picasa entry in this list) and YouTube host videos. Picasa is more for personal storage and YouTube is more for public display. You can use either service, but one possible strategy is to put all your videos on Picasa, and put only selected ones that you want to display broadly on YouTube.

TIP: **See What Google Thinks About Google Services**

You can find additional information about Google's view of how its services work together in Google's Help area, in an article called "Make Google Products Work for You." The article is at http://www.google.com/support/bin/static.py?page=guide.cs&guide=25765&topic=25766.

You won't start using all these services, all the time, at once. You should try, though, to adopt all those that make sense; your business will probably become one of, if not the most, online-savvy among your competition.

Summary

In this lesson, you set up a Google account for your business, preferably by creating a Gmail account. You chose your Gmail login name and learned about other Google services that can help your business grow.

LESSON 5

Claiming Your Google Places Page

In this lesson, you learn how to find your Google Places page, or start a new one if Google hasn't done so. You then learn how to add or edit your business information, including contact information, location, service area, and hours of operation. Finally, you learn how to verify your Google Places listing to gain exclusive access to it.

Finding (or Not Finding) Your Page

The first step in working on your Google Places page is to find out whether you already have one created for you by Google. You can see a description of the contents of a Google Places page in Lesson 1, "Introducing Google Places," and a description of how to edit basic information fields—without having to verify your ownership first—in Lesson 2, "Editing Your Google Places Page."

If your business already has a Google Places page, assembled for you by Google, this might come as a surprise to you. Having a preassembled page is almost entirely good news. Not only can customers find basic information about your business easily in Google Search and Google Maps, they can also see that your business is important and a real business by the fact that people are talking about you online (as shown on your Google Places page), listing you in directories (as shown on your Google Places page), and so on.

However, you might be surprised, or even disappointed and frustrated, by some of the content on your existing Google Places page. Google gathers information about your business from all over the Web, and if that information includes negative comments, they might show up on your page.

This happens whether the comments are fair or unfair. In most cases, Google will not do anything about negative comments for you. See Lesson 7, "Adding Photos," for some steps you can take to help yourself.

On the other hand, you might not be surprised or disappointed to find that you do *not* already have a Google Places page. Your business might or might not have a business license, be listed in various directories such as the phone directory and online listings, and so on. Sometimes your business just doesn't get Google's attention; other times, Google messes up, and even puts a different business at your business address. Again, see Lesson 7 for steps you can take to help yourself.

If you're not already listed, adding your page can immediately attract related content from other sites, if your business is mentioned on any. Or, it might take a while for the information to show up on your new Google Places page. You might have to make explicit efforts to get listed in some of the directories that Google takes information from to then have that information show up in your Google Places page.

If you need to create a new Google Places page, follow the steps in the "Adding a New Listing" section, later in this lesson, and then proceed through the rest of the lesson. If you have an existing page that you haven't claimed yet as your own, skip the next section and go straight to the following section, "Editing Your Listing." In either case, work your way through to the final section, "Verifying Your Listing."

Deciding What to Add First

Adding your business to Google, or editing and verifying your existing listing, is an exciting step. It's also quite easy, although the verification process, described later in this lesson, does tend to make people a bit nervous. It's hardly ever a problem. (If your business or practices don't fit Google's policies and procedures, as described in Lesson 7, verification might pose a problem.)

The information that you enter for your Google Pages listing is used for not only the listing itself. Google uses the information to suck in other information from around the Web for your Google Places page, and to index your Google Places page for use by Google's search engine and other tools.

Therefore, it's important to get the information that you enter right the first time, and correct every time you update it, to as great an extent as you can. Take care to get the information right as you go along, and don't be afraid to break off the process of adding information if you need to do research or think something over before proceeding.

There are three kinds of fields in your listing:

- **Basic business information:** This is made up of name, location, contact information, description, and category. You can edit this information even before you claim your page, as described in Lesson 2. Detailed information on these fields is given in this lesson.

- **Extended information:** This is open hours, service area, and payment options, plus photos, videos, and custom fields. I suggest you enter the first few fields in detail now, as described in this lesson. However, you should consider leaving most of your work with photos, videos, and custom fields until later. (Details for these fields are given in later lessons.)

  That way, you can let Google go out and find any such information that's already on the Web for you. You can then dedicate your own efforts to complementing and extending—or even correcting—the impression that visitors to your Google Places page get from the additional information that Google finds.

- **Marketing information and offers:** Coupons, real-time updates, and QR codes make up this kind of information. You can't create these marketing tools until after your site is verified, as described in this lesson. Later lessons in this book tell you how to make these additions.

After you enter the basics, and verify your listing, Google will publish your listing, and also gather any information it can find from around the Web, including photos, possibly videos, and maps.

This is a good time to add your own extended information. When you're sure your listing is solid, you can then add marketing information and offers, as described in later lessons in this book.

Bringing Up Your Business Listing

If you are creating a brand-new listing, you have to go through a couple of extra steps. If your business is already listed by Google, getting the listing onscreen is easier. In either case, follow these steps:

1. If you don't have one already, create a Google account.

   You can use a personal Google account to create your business listing, but I recommend that you create an account specifically for use by the business. See Lesson 4, "Signing Up for a Google Account," for specifics.

2. Try to find your business on Google Places, as described in Lesson 2. If you find it, skip to the next section, "Adding or Editing Basic Information." If you don't find your business on Google Places, go to the next step.

3. Open a web browser and go to the Google Places page at http://www.google.com/places.

   The Google Places page appears, as shown in Figure 5.1. You will see this page only if you are not signed into a Google account that is associated with a business listed on Google Places. If so, go ahead and sign in.

4. Click the **Add New Business** button.

   The Google Places page for adding basic business information appears. It's almost the same as the page for editing an existing listing. Both are described in the next section.

TIP: **Look Out for Misteaks**

Double-check for misspellings and typos as you go along, in the Name and Address fields and other fields. I recently helped edit a company website that misspelled the word *public* in a particularly embarrassing way.

FIGURE 5.1   Here's where you start your Google Places adventure.

Adding or Editing Basic Information

What I'm calling basic information for Google Places does seem pretty basic: business name, address, phone, email address, website, description, and categories.

If you are creating a new listing, you enter this basic information in the first web page that appears. If you are editing an existing listing, this basic information appears first in a longer web page.

CAUTION: **Log into the Correct Account**

Make sure you are logged into the Google account that you want to use for your business for all steps of adding, editing, and verifying your business information. The Google account you use will be the one through which you enter the PIN code that ties your Google Places business information to a specific account, as mentioned at the end of this lesson.

Follow the steps in the previous section to bring up the entry screen for basic Google Places information. Then follow these steps to enter or edit it, as shown in Figure 5.2.

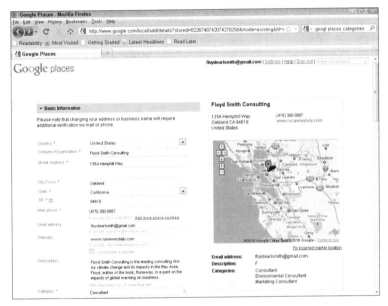

FIGURE 5.2   Tell Google Places where your business is located.

1. Enter or edit the name and address of your business.

    As you enter address information, the map will display a marker, and pan and zoom to show the marker's location close up.

    It's quite common for address information to be incorrect for large sites, and not unheard of for smaller ones.

2. If the marker location is incorrect, click the **Fix Incorrect Marker Location** link. Follow the instructions onscreen to get the marker location right.

    A dialog will appear, as shown in Figure 5.3, to enable you to move the marker location. For a large site, such as a national park, you might have to pan and zoom quite a bit to get the right location. You might also want to consult with others about the right spot to direct visitors to.

FIGURE 5.3 You can help get Google's maps right for your business.

3. Enter or edit your business phone number.

It's best if this number has the same area code and even exchange—the first three digits of a seven-digit local phone number—as other nearby businesses. This reassures customers that you're truly local.

4. Click the **Add More Phone Numbers** link if you want to list an alternative phone, mobile phone, fax number, and/or TTY/TDD for use by deaf people. Then enter the additional numbers.

It's traditional for a business to have a single, land-line number (not a mobile phone number). However, you should add additional numbers if it will help people reach you in a way that you're ready to be reached.

For instance, if you add a mobile phone number, you help people reach you off hours and send text messages to you. However, you also enable them to call you at 3 a.m. with a seemingly urgent message, delivered in another language or with a strong accent, from some distant part of the world. Be sure you're ready for this. If you give a fax number, be sure you can always have the fax machine ready, with paper and toner in it. If you're not ready for the possible hassles, it's best not to list that specific type of number.

5. Enter or edit your business email address.

This is a tough one; entering a personal email address looks a bit informal and unprofessional, whereas entering something official-looking, such as info@mybiz.com, looks intimidating—and implies that the email might not get an answer anytime soon. A name such as manager@mybiz.com might send just the right impression. See Lesson 4 for information about how to sign up for a Google email account, which you can customize to forward mail to your usual account.

6. Enter or edit your company website address, if you have one and want to bring it to the attention of Google Places visitors at this time. If not, click the **I Don't Have a Website** check box.

It's good to have a company website, but you should send people to it only if it's good-looking, up-to-date, and accurate enough to reflect well on you.

7. Enter a description of your business, as shown in Figure 5.2, up to 200 characters.

This description is important marketing copy, but it should be written in plain English, simply describing your business. It should read as if it were written by an independent observer, although not a particularly critical one. The description text can also help with search engine optimization (SEO) for your business.

8. Enter or edit the categories in which your business belongs. To add additional categories, click the **Add Another Category** link.

Enter up to five categories that are appropriate for your business. You can enter category names as they occur to you; as you type, Google uses your partial entry to display suggestions in a scrolling list. You must enter at least one category that matches one of the suggestions. You can also enter custom category names, or use the list in Appendix A, "Places Categories," to use the category names suggested by Google. See Appendix A for a complete discussion.

9. If you are entering a new listing, you'll be finished with the first page, and have the opportunity to click the Submit button. If you are happy with the information you have added so far, click **Submit**. If you aren't, click the **Sign Out** link in the upper-right corner of your screen to terminate the process.

If you click Submit, Google creates your business listing. The next screen will enable you to add additional details. When you click Submit on that screen, the additional details are added to your listing.

If you click **Sign Out**, however, all your changes will be lost, including any categories you have entered.

CAUTION: **Think Before You Submit**

Google creates your business listing when you click the Submit button at the end of the first page of data that you enter. If you want to start over, you can delete a listing, as described in Lesson 7; however, it takes Google about four weeks to process the deletion. With this in mind, think carefully before you click Submit.

If you are creating the listing for the first time, and want to be clever, you can open another browser window or tab and go to http://www.google. com/places. You should see a list with the business listing you just created in it. Quickly close the browser window or tab to avoid confusing Google's databases by entering similar information from two places at once.

Adding In-Depth Information to Your Listing

After you submit the initial screen of information about your business, as described in the previous steps, Google creates your listing. Google then offers you another screen in which you can add more information. If you are continuing with editing an existing entry, these fields simply continue on from the ones described in the previous section.

The fields you can enter include the following:

▶ Service Areas and Location Settings

▶ Open Hours (Hours of Operation)

▶ Payment Options

▶ Photos

▶ Videos

▶ Additional Details

Service areas are of particular interest. For most locally based businesses, such as a grocery store, you list an address and people come to you. However, if you deliver, you'll want to show your delivery area. If you don't have a storefront—for instance, if you have a home-based advice, coaching, or consultancy business—you cannot list your business address, but you can still list the area you serve.

> CAUTION: **Service Areas Are Not Always Seen**
> When users see your business listing in Google Places, they are given the option, **Show Service Area**, to turn on the display of your service area. Users might not turn on the service area option, and might call without having seen whether you serve their location. See Lesson 3, "Using Google Places," for an example.

Service areas take two forms. One is a circular area around your business address, as shown in Figure 5.4. This is great for businesses such as pizza delivery that have an explicit or implicit time commitment. Or, you might want to drive only 40 miles, say, to reach a client. Circular service areas are a bit tough on customers, though, because they think of themselves as living in specific towns and cities, not within circles drawn around your business.

FIGURE 5.4   A circular service area might be more convenient for you than your customers.

The other, more interesting kind of service area is a kind of blob made up of specific cities, towns, and ZIP codes near you. This is shown in Figure 5.5. Google Places fills in the areas in-between to form an odd kind of shape.

For example, for my consulting work, my service area is parts of the San Francisco Bay Area served by BART and CalTrain, and within about an hour and a half of me. I was able to specify this by naming just three points—San Jose, San Francisco, and Richmond—in the northern part of the East Bay.

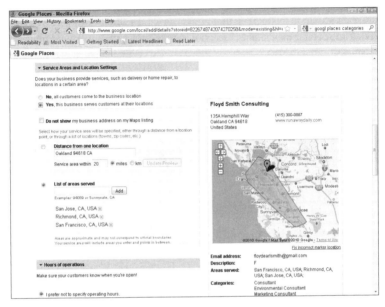

FIGURE 5.5   Enter a circular or irregular service area.

If I meet potentially high-value new clients who live outside those areas, I still do business with them, but only if the rewards seem worth the hassle. For people who find me on Google Places, I find that people outside the service area still call me—but I have the option of turning them down if the business isn't worth the trouble.

> TIP: **Be Ready to Serve**
>
> Show only the service area that you really want to serve—where it's easy and affordable for you to serve new customers. You can still serve existing customers, and high-value new customers, outside your service area.

However, whether this is a new listing or an existing one, you will not have verified the listing yet. I recommend that you enter in only the first three types of information, which are somewhat basic: service area and location, open hours, and payment options. I recommend you then verify your listing, as described in the last section in this chapter, "Verifying Your Listing." When that's done, you can spend more time on the additional fields, some of which can require a fair amount of time and effort.

Follow these steps to add more in-depth information to your listing:

1. Specify whether customers come to your business location or the business serves customers at their locations.

    This is a tricky one. Only a minority of businesses, such as many pizza parlors, routinely offer delivery service for the general public. However, many businesses will do deliveries for big customers, shut-ins, and so on—perhaps for an extra fee, and perhaps only after regular business hours.

    I recommend that you consider describing your business as serving customers at their location, even if you only do it in restricted circumstances. When customers ask you about it, you can explain the circumstances to them.

    If you enter Yes to service areas and location settings, Google will bring up a dialog and a map to enable you to enter your service area, as shown in Figure 5.5.

2. If you answered **No** to service areas and location settings, go to the next step. If you entered **Yes**, enter the details, including whether to show your business address on your Maps listing and the areas served. Click the **Distance from One Location** radio button to create a circular area based on a ZIP code, plus a radius around it. (Click the **Update Preview** button to see the area depicted on a map.) Click the other radio button, **List of Areas Served**, to enter a list of areas served; for each area, enter the name, and then click **Add**. Repeat until you've entered all areas. See the beginning of this section for more on service areas.

    For the option of entering areas served, Google warns you that areas entered are approximate. Google includes points between the areas you specify, forming a contiguous, albeit irregular, blob, as shown in Figure 5.6.

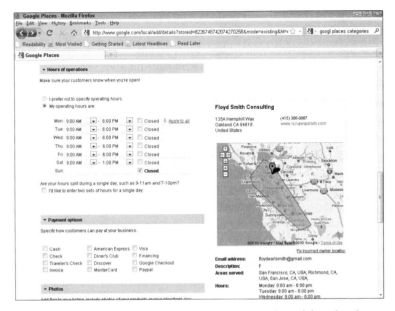

FIGURE 5.6   You can easily specify a lunch break and special weekend hours.

3. For hours of operation, choose the radio button for not specifying your hours of operation or the button for listing them. If you choose the latter, use the pull-downs to specify your hours, as shown in Figure 5.6. You can enter Monday hours—click the **Apply to All** link to apply them throughout the week—then customize any days that are different. To enter split shifts—for instance, open from 9 a.m. to 5 p.m., but closed for lunch from 12 noon to 1 p.m.—click the **I'd Like to Enter Two Sets of Hours for a Single Day** check box to set it. Then enter the second set of hours for the days that have them.

Open hours are really, really important to many customers. Part of your value add as a local business is convenience, and publicizing your open hours are a big part of this. Remember that, in many cases, you're competing with other local businesses that might be open more hours, and possibly also with online shopping options that are open all the time. So, carefully specify the broadest opening hours that you can responsibly commit to, and then stick to them.

4. Click the check boxes for all the payment options you accept: cash, check, traveler's check, invoice, American Express, Diner's Club, Discover, MasterCard, Visa, Financing, Google Checkout, and PayPal.

    As with delivery, there's a potential problem here: You might want to offer some customers more payment options than others. For payment, I recommend that you list only the payment options that you're comfortable offering to everyone, and then negotiate if asked for additional options.

5. If you choose, use the Additional Details area (see Lesson 6), the Photos area (see Lesson 7), and the **Videos** area (see Lesson 8) to add more content to your Google Places page.

    You can add this kind of content now, but I recommend that you wait to see what Google finds for you after you've had your listing up for a little bit first. Also, using these areas properly might require a bit of education and thought, so consider delaying these additions for now and adding them after reviewing the relevant lessons later in this book.

6. Check all the choices you've entered, and then click **Submit**.

    Google will add the information to your listing, and then request that you verify the listing, as described in the next section.

TIP: **Try To Meet Customer Expectations**

Try to offer the same open hours as other local businesses near you, even if you're not a traditional type of local business—if you're a consultancy, for instance. People form deeply ingrained habits about when they expect to be able to do business locally, and you should meet their expectations. This cuts two ways: Being open extra-long hours might not do you much good if no one expects you to be open extra early or extra late, resulting in little additional business during the extra opening hours.

Verifying Your Listing

Google contacts you to make sure that the Gmail account you use when creating your Google Places listing is the one that should be associated with your business data.

Google, unfortunately, calls this *validating* your listing in some places and *verifying* it in others. I like the word *verify* better, so I'm going to use it, but don't be surprised to also see the word *validate* used to mean the same thing.

Google can verify your listing in two ways: over the phone or by sending you a postcard. The phone technique is much easier—it only takes a few minutes. If you use the postcard option, it takes two to three weeks.

Follow these steps to verify your listing:

1. Follow the earlier steps to bring up the option to validate, or verify, your listing, as shown in Figure 5.7.

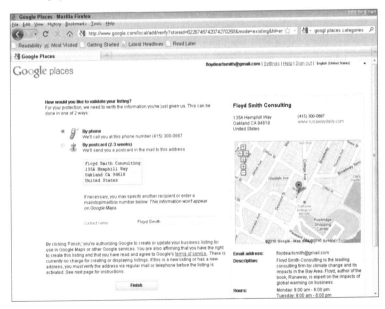

FIGURE 5.7   Get ready to verify your ownership.

For a business that is not yet in Google Places, follow the steps described earlier in this lesson. Alternatively, go to the Google home page, sign in to your account, and choose **Settings**, and then **Google Places**. Your Google Places dashboard will appear; click the **Verify Ownership** link.

For a business that already is in Google Places, find the business in Google Maps, as described in Lesson 2. Click the **Business Owner** link. Choose **Edit My Business** Information and click **Continue**. Edit the fields, as described in the previous sections of this lesson, and click **Submit**.

2. Choose a radio button for the update: By Phone or By Postcard (2–3 weeks).

   Phone verification is very quick; a computer calls your business phone number and gives you a five-digit PIN code in just a few minutes. Postcard verification is very slow. (It's pretty secure, though; other people might see the code, but they can't log in to your Google account to get it.)

3. Click **Finish**.

   After you click Finish, your Dashboard will appear. If you are using the phone verification, just wait; for postcard verification, return to the Dashboard when you receive the postcard.

   If you choose phone verification, a computer will call you and tell you the code. If you don't answer the phone, Google will not give you the entire code in a message; you have to answer the phone to get the whole code. Be sure to write it down someplace safe! For postcard verification, you'll get a postcard 2–3 weeks later. You will need the PIN only once; after that, your Google account password will serve as security for your information.

4. In the Dashboard, enter the PIN code.

   The PIN will be accepted. You will have full access to all the functionality of Google Places for your business. Congratulations!

From this point on, your business information can be edited only by some-one logged in to the Google account from which the listing was verified. No one else can change your business information.

TIP: **Cheaper by the Dozen?**

Google Places offers ways to upload information for several loca-tions at once, which is very useful if you have a franchise or similar structure. For more information, visit http://www.google.com/support/places/bin/static.py?page=guide.cs&guide=28247&topic=28291.

Summary

In this lesson, you learned how to find or start a Google Places page. You learned how to add or edit business information, including contact infor-mation, location, service area, and hours of operation. You then learned how to verify your Google Places listing, and did so, gaining exclusive access to it.

LESSON 6

Improving Your Google Places Page

In this lesson, you learn how to add custom fields called Additional Details to your page. You also learn highlights of the Comment Posting policy for Google Places reviews, the quality guidelines for listings, and the local listings content policy.

Adding New Features to Your Listing

Google Places supports all sorts of must-have features for your online presence, such as contact information and driving directions, as described in Lesson 5, "Claiming Your Google Places Page." It also enables you to add any kind of label you want and a value to match. You can add an email address, describe parking availability—even list the name of a specific employee, such as a receptionist or chef.

> TIP: **Use Additional Details**
>
> Adding Additional Details to your listing is a great way to introduce terms onto your Google Places page that improve your search engine optimization (SEO) results. See Lesson 14, "Improving Search Engine Results," for details.

The idea is to give brief, factual information. "Recommended by: all the top local newspapers" doesn't work; "Recommended by: *SF Guardian, SFGate*" does, especially if you link to the comments in question.

Don't brag; most of the information should be data (that is, neutral facts, although you can select positive features of your business). Use nouns as the label names, followed by neutral descriptions—worded as if they were provided by a disinterested third party. You can link to positive wording, but it's disconcerting to the visitor to your Google Places page to see ad-type copy on your Google Places page.

TIP: **Ask Disabled Customers to Call**

Encourage disabled customers to call you (deaf customers will usually have special phones that translate their typing to speech, and vice versa). First, you can discuss accessibility with customers so that they can either visit you with confidence (and on a day and time when you can be most helpful) or discuss other options. You can help customers shop over the phone and discuss delivery options, and any associated charges, as well as other ways to meet needs that you can't handle.

One possible exception is reviews. If a reviewer said "best pizza in town," and the Reviews information that Google puts on your page doesn't include it, you might want to. For example: "Reviews: 'Best pizza in town' – *SF Guardian*." You'd want to link the quote to the specific review online. (If it's not still available, put a page summarizing the review on your website and link to that.)

A powerful boost to this feature is provided by the fact that a label can be a hyperlink. So, if your business is part of a chain, you can not only provide the name of the chain, you can link to its home page—but always link to the most relevant specific page you can.

You can use this feature to provide useful, detailed information, of course, but also for marketing purposes. One technique that I recommend businesses use is something I call *borrowing credibility*. You tie your business to a well-known, or at least worthy-sounding, group or other resource. It's sort of the opposite of guilt by association.

By mentioning the name of a chain you belong to, or a professional association, you wrap yourself in the flag of that organization's place in your potential customer's mind. This effect is only enhanced by linking to the organization in question. Even if customers never click the link, they know that you're happy for them to do so, and to see for themselves what the organization you're associated with is all about.

Google offers a long list of labels, including industry-specific labels, shown in Figure 6.1. You can see the list at http://www.google.com/support/places/bin/answer.py?answer=182238&cbid=182238&src=cb&lev=index.

FIGURE 6.1 Google helps you out with ideas for additional details for your Places page.

Here are some ideas for labels, with a few borrowed from the Google list, plus some original ideas:

▶ **Chain:** Sample values: Peet's Coffee; Best Western Hotels. Your memberships in a chain or other kind of grouping that shares marketing expenses, resources, and so on.

- ▶ **Disabled accessibility:** Sample values: Yes; No, but call for shopping and delivery options. See the Tip for details.

- ▶ **Online ordering:** Sample value: http://www.yoursite.com/shopping. Provide a full URL, in case the customer wants to write it down or save it in a document. Then link it to a shopping page on your website.

- ▶ **Memberships:** Sample values: Oakland Business Association; Project Managers Association. Any association memberships that bolster your credibility to provide the goods or services that you advertise.

- ▶ **Certifications:** Sample value: CPA. Relatively well-known professional certifications that bolster your credibility to provide the goods/services that you advertise.

- ▶ **Clients:** Sample values: Sears; First National Bank. Current or past clients who are willing to be listed in your Google Places page.

TIP: **Think About What Labels to Add**

Yellow Pages ads, websites (your own, and competitors'), and advertisements are all good places to look for ideas as to what custom labels to provide. Another source is customer questions. If someone asks you a question in person, for instance, there's a good chance that someone sitting behind a computer is wondering the same thing.

Follow these steps to add additional details:

1. Go to http://www.google.com and sign in to the Google account associated with your business. Choose **Settings**, **Google Account Settings**. From the list of Google products that appears, choose **Google Places**.

Your Google Places Dashboard opens, as shown in Figure 6.2.

When you go to find Google Places in your list of services, you might notice that some Google services are called *Google* <service>, whereas others are just called <service>, with the Google implied. You just have to get used to the choice Google makes when finding a given service.

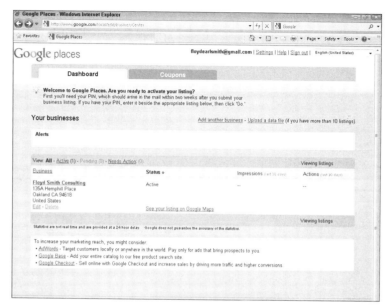

FIGURE 6.2 Your Dashboard will be bare at first, but busier soon enough.

2. For the site you want to update, click **Edit**.

Your Google Places information page opens.

TIP: **Collapse Completed Areas**

You can collapse and expand areas on the Google Places editing page for your business, as shown in Figure 6.3. Just click the triangle to the left of the name of the area, such as Payment Options or Photos. I recommend that you collapse empty areas and leave areas where you've made entries expanded, as a prompt to edit any information that needs to be changed.

---

3. Scroll to the bottom of the page to find the Additional Details area, as shown in Figure 6.3.

A couple of examples and a couple of empty text boxes appear.

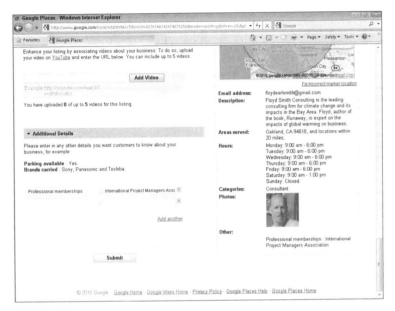

FIGURE 6.3   Additional Details make your page richer.

4. Enter a category name in the first text box, such as Professional memberships. Press **Tab**.

   A couple of examples and a couple of empty text boxes appear.

TIP: **Do It Google's Way**

Google uses mostly lowercase for prompts (for instance, Email address, not Email Address). So, you should too, for consistency; use Professional memberships, not Professional Memberships.

---

5. Enter details that go with the category name, such as International Project Managers Association. Press **Tab**.

6. To open up another pair of category name/value(s) text entry boxes, click the **Add Another** link. Continue adding category names and values.

Another pair of empty text boxes open up, and the Category name/values pair that you just entered shows up in the preview box to the right, as shown in Figure 6.3.

7. To delete a category name/values pair, click the **X** to the right of the pair.

   The category name and values disappear from the entry area and from the preview to the right.

8. When you've finished entering additional details, click **Submit**.

   The editing page for your listing closes. If you haven't already validated your listing, you're taken to the page that prompts you to do so. Follow the instructions in Lesson 5 to validate your listing. Otherwise, you're taken to the Dashboard.

Google Places Policies

Google Places has a full set of policies that all users of the service are expected to follow. Google can remove content that doesn't follow its policies, and can even ban users from making certain types of postings, or close a user's Google account, if its policies are flouted energetically enough.

Google has four relevant types of policies for you and others to follow:

▶ **Comment posting policy:** Covers reviews users leave on your Google Places page.

▶ **Quality guidelines:** Specify the requirements for your business's Google Places listing.

▶ **Local listings content policy:** Bans certain kinds of statements in your listing.

▶ **Coupon guidelines:** Specify what you can and can't do in coupons you create (see Lesson 9, "Adding Coupons").

The coupon guidelines are discussed in Lesson 9. The comment posting policy, quality guidelines, and local listings content policy are briefly described next. For full listings of all policies, see http://www.google.com/support/places/bin/topic.py?hl=en&topic=28094.

> TIP: **Google Controls Removing "Bad" Reviews**
>
> Google doesn't try to directly manage all the user-generated content, such as Google Places reviews, that graces its many web pages. Instead, it depends on users to report problem content that might violate its policies. Google might then investigate the complaint and take action, such as removing the offending content. To learn how to report problematic reviews for possible action, see Lesson 13, "Using QR Codes and Getting Better Reviews."

Comment Posting Policy

The comment posting policy covers reviews that users of Google places make on your business's Places page.

You want to encourage reviews, as described in Lesson 13, "Using QR Codes and Getting Better Reviews," but you should know what the rules are, in case someone breaks them in reviewing your business. Some of the *don'ts* include the following:

- ▶ Fake reviews intended to manipulate ratings up or down
- ▶ Sexually explicit or profane content and links
- ▶ Abusive, hateful, threatening, or harassing content and links
- ▶ Files with viruses and so on, and links to them
- ▶ Copyright and IP violations, and misrepresentation
- ▶ Violation of applicable laws and regulations
- ▶ Advertisements masquerading as comments

Google also recommends that comments be useful, informative, honest, balanced, easy to read, grammatically correct, and "nice."

The comment posting policy can be found at http://www.google.com/support/places/bin/answer.py?hl=en&answer=141379. You should, in theory, be able to get comments that violate the policy removed from your site.

Unfortunately, however, this page does not include links to getting comments that might be in violation—let alone comments that you simply don't like—removed. See Lesson 13 for details.

TIP: **It's Hard Work to Improve Your Reviews**
The comment posting policy for Google Places does not cover comments that Google scrapes from other sites, such as Yelp.com and places on your Google Places page. To get rid of such comments, you need to appeal to the site owner of the site from which the comments come. If you're successful in getting the comment removed from the original site, you then need to wait until Google updates the feed from that site and removes its copy of the offending quote from your Google Places page.

Quality Guidelines

Quality guidelines cover the *shoulds* for your Google Places business listings. There is so much content on Google that it might be unlikely for your page to be cited if you break them. However, if you follow the policies, you'll have a better and more reliable Google Places page, and users will appreciate it—and, quite possibly, be more likely to patronize your business.

Following the shoulds is also likely to help your search engine rankings, in subtle but important ways. Google is constantly changing its search engine algorithms to improve results for users and foil people who try to manipulate the results. Many of the shoulds listed here are things that Google's algorithms can detect and use to enhance or reduce your place in search results in Google Search, Google Maps, and elsewhere.

The guidelines include the following:

▶ Owners and authorized representatives are the only ones who should verify a listing.

▶ The business name and contact details should match offline representations; no additional keywords, description information, phone numbers, URLs, or other information crammed in there to help search results and search engine rankings.

▶ Only create one listing per overall service area, not per city, town, or ZIP code. Also only one listing per doctor's office, lawyer's office, and so on—not one listing per specialty.

▶ Provide a direct phone number and a specific URL for the specific business and address listed.

▶ Use a shared business email account if you want to allow multiple users to update your listing. Also, use an email account whose domain name matches the domain name of your business's website (see Lesson 4, "Signing Up for a Google Account").

The quality guidelines can be found at http://www.google.com/support/places/bin/answer.py?hl=en&answer=107528. There is no stated policy for not following them, but your Google search engine ranking could certainly be at risk if you don't.

CAUTION: **Follow Google's Rules**

Google will ban businesses from its search results if it concludes that its search results are being manipulated. None of the how-to steps in this book constitute manipulation, but tricks such as putting your business phone number in the same Google Places field as your business name might. Be very careful before you bend, let alone break, the rules.

Local Listings Content Policy

The content in your Google Places page should follow guidelines similar to the preceding Comment Posting guidelines, including the following:

▶ No nudity, obscenity, or sexually explicit material.

▶ No hate speech and no violent or bullying behavior reflected in your content.

▶ No impersonating others, and no sharing others' private or confidential information; no violating their intellectual property rights.

▶ No breaking the law.

▶ No spam, malicious content, fake reviews, links to other "stuff," or advertisements masquerading as comments.

▶ Reviews should be about the business in question and not manipulative (that is, not intended simply to raise or lower rankings).

The local listings content policy can be found at http://www.google.com/support/places/bin/answer.py?hl=en&answer=176519.

TIP: **It's Easy for Users to Report Problems**

There is an easy way for users who don't like your listing to complain; a Report a Problem link is available on every Google Places page.

Summary

In this lesson, you learned how to add additional details to your page and reviewed highlights of the comment posting policy, the quality guidelines for listings, and the local listings content policy.

Adding Photos

In this lesson, you learn how photos enhance your Google Places page. You learn how to take suitable photos, how to process photos on your computer for use online, how to follow Google Places rules for photos, how to add pictures to your Google Places page from your computer or Picasa web albums, and how to delete photos.

Adding Photos to Your Places Page

I spent a couple of years working on company magazines for employees, and photos of people were so important, the formula for a successful magazine was called "people on pages." Your Google Places page should be the same way. People want to see photos, especially of the people who will greet them if they call or come by.

Getting at least a few decent photos onto your Google Places page should be a priority. Photos will make your page stand out—to pop from the clutter on a typical user's screen and get attention. You should get photos onto your page as soon as possible after it launches.

> TIP: **Move Fast on Photos**
>
> Don't wait for photos to be available before claiming and updating your Google Places page, as described in previous lessons. But after your page is claimed and updated, add photos to it as soon as possible.

Paul Marcus, owner of the eponymous Paul Marcus Wines, was very lucky. As you can see from the business's Google Places page in Figure 1.2, before he even claimed his Google Places page, Google had found a photo of him and stuck it on the page. Just that one old, black-and-white photograph brought that very basic Places page to life.

You probably haven't been so lucky. Even if Google generated a Google Places page for you, it probably doesn't have any photos on it—and, even if it does, not very good ones.

Plan on getting some photos up on your Google Places page using the information and steps in this lesson. Photos are likely to bring you more customers, no question about it.

Photos are also much more important than video. Only a minority of customers will bother to play a video. Everyone who visits your Google Places page or the pages of your website sees the photos on it.

NOTE: **Photos and Videos Are Popular**

At the time of this writing, the "Add Photos and Videos" article on the Google Places help site for owners is the second most popular article, showing the importance of the topic (and of this lesson). To see the online article, visit http://www.google.com/support/places/bin/answer.py?answer=75566&src=top5&lev=answer.

Here are a few suggestions for using photos:

▶ **Use five to seven photos:** The average person can remember five to seven things in short-term memory, and often won't bother with more items than that. So, consider adding about half a dozen photos. (Google Places currently has a limit of 10.)

▶ **Choose from five types of photos:** There are five types of photos you should include, in order of importance: the owner or top manager, other staff, the premises, products, and customers.

▶ **Get a pro in:** Professional photographers know how to make you, your staff, your site, and your "stuff" look good. (The big secret is using enough light.) You should be able to find someone good locally for not too much money for online-only quality, and you can get photos taken for your website, as well.

▶ **Don't get stale:** Update your photos at least every six months or so, and add a photo whenever something cool happens, such as a

big display for the holidays or getting an award. If you have a
bunch of good photos beyond your top half a dozen, put them on
your website or a business Flickr or Picasa account.

> TIP: **Photos Help All Around**
>
> Photos on your Google Places page can help with your search
> engine results, clickthroughs by users from search results to your
> site (rather than a competitor's), and more. See Lesson 14,
> "Improving Search Engine Results," for details.

Taking Good Photos

I know I said "use a pro" earlier, but no one can have a pro available all
the time—and some of you are going to do it all yourself anyway. Even if
you do use a pro, you should know what good work is. Here are some tips
for taking good photos for use online:

▶ **Trip the light fantastic:** No one is going to stare into the murky
depths of some crummy online photo to try to figure out
whether the subject is a face or a fish. Light everything brightly,
as in Figure 7.1. Use Photoshop to try to lighten the image if it's
too dark.

▶ **Keep the light behind you:** Don't put people in front of a sunny
window and expect to be able to see their faces or much else.
Your subjects—whether people or objects—should have the
brightest light around in their faces, not behind them.

▶ **Focus on the shock of the new:** Product shots are easy, and often
the manufacturer or supplier will give you good ones for free. You
can get shots of your premises taken once and keep rotating them
forever. Get in the habit of photographing the things that change:
staff, customers, special events, and new displays.

▶ **Take lots and lots of (digital) shots:** Film is fairly expensive
these days, but space on the memory card of a digital camera is
just about free. Take a lot of (well-lit) shots and hope for a bit
of serendipity in terms of catching a nice smile or a friendly
interaction.

FIGURE 7.1   A good online photo is simple and well lit.

In addition to taking good photos, you can also *make* good photos. A lot of the photographer's art these days happens in Photoshop or a similar program, not when the picture is taken. So, again, you can do a lot yourself, or at least school yourself so that you can judge how well a professional's work is serving your needs.

> TIP: **A Little Help from Your Friends**
>
> If you don't know what some of the suggestions in this section mean, find friends or colleagues who know a bit about digital photography and show them the part that's confusing you. The concepts here are widely known, and you should be able to get a good explanation, or perhaps, if you're lucky, even a good demonstration.

Here are some tips for making photos work well online:

▶ **Keep it simple:** Online photos are very small and have very few pixels per inch—perhaps 100 pixels per inch, compared to at least 300 for a magazine photo, and more than a thousand for a traditional photograph. So, keep your online photos simple.

- ▶ **Keep copies:** Save a high-resolution, uncropped version of your photo off on to some separate storage medium before you start hacking away at it. Better to have to do a half an hour or so of rework than to lose a valuable original entirely.

- ▶ **Crop tightly:** Online photos seem to get cropped ever tighter with time, and rightly so. The photos are too small and low resolution to be worth looking at for long, so the subject of the photo has to pop right out to be seen fully at a quick glance.

- ▶ **Resize your photos:** Your photo-editing program will have the ability to resize your photo from the many hundreds of dots per inch of a high-resolution digital photo to the 100 dots per inch or so needed for onscreen display. This makes the file size much, much smaller without any visible loss of quality.

- ▶ **Compress lightly:** Enough people have fast Internet connections these days that it's okay to compress smaller photos down to perhaps 25KB or a bit less and larger ones to just under 60KB. These fatter files give a warmer appearance and are easier to look at.

- ▶ **Get permission:** These days, people are quite sensitive about permission, especially if their photograph is used for commercial purposes. You can just about assume it's okay to use pictures of your employees in most jurisdictions, but if you want to include customers or other outsiders, get a model release.

It's not only faces you have to be careful of; trademark and copyright holders can also be sensitive about use of their intellectual property. If a wine shop shows a close-up of a bottle of wine on its site, for instance, the winemaker might want to have a release form signed first, allowing the use of the trademark. (This isn't them being jerks; their lawyers may tell them that they have to create and enforce such policies to protect their rights.) You may have to consult a lawyer to know what's protected and what isn't; for instance, even the famous curvy shape of a classic Coke bottle has been held to be protected.

Following the Rules

Google Places has a few rules for how you can use photos in your Google Places listing. They're pretty simple, and not entirely helpful:

- **Keep photos smaller than 1MB:** You have an upper limit as to file size of 1MB per photo. But don't actually use photos anywhere near this large, or your Google Places page might take several minutes to fully load on a slow modem or a bad cell phone connection. 100KB per photo is plenty.

- **Keep photos smaller than 1024 × 1024 pixels:** At this size, a single photo takes up just about the whole screen on a computer, and more than the whole screen on an iPad, let alone on a mobile phone. Think of small photos as being smaller than 100 × 100 pixels, and large ones as being smaller than 200 × 200 pixels. Figure 7.2 shows these image sizes on a 1024 × 768 resolution screen (the size of an iPad screen or a small computer screen).

FIGURE 7.2   Photos in 100 × 100 pixels or 200 × 200 pixels of space give you—and your Google Places page visitors—enough room to work.

- **Use JPG, GIF, PNG, TIFF, or BMP files:** No one would use BMP or TIFF files for online photos of this type; they're huge in file size and to no benefit for this purpose. Use JPEG compression.

> **NOTE: More About JPEGs**
>
> The acronym JPEG stands for Joint Photographic Experts Group. The JPEG standard does a great job of compressing photos in a way that makes them much smaller in file size (easily 90% smaller than the original) with little compromise in the appearance of the image to the viewer. You can compress an image more than 90% using JPEG, but the quality of the image is likely to degrade quickly as you up the compression percentage beyond 90% or so. Experiment with each image to find out what you can get away with.

▶ **Use Picasa web albums:** Google makes it easy to add photos that are already online to your Google Places page, but only if the photos are on Google's Picasa website. This is a major hassle for the millions of people who use Flickr, the most popular site of its type, but of course Google will use its own services when it can. Use Picasa's tools to create a photo of a smaller image size and file size, as recommended in the previous section, before you import it from Picasa.

Adding a Picture from Your Computer

Google Places makes it quite easy to add a picture from your computer or Picasa Web Albums to the Google Places page for your business. To add a picture from your computer, just follow these steps:

1. Take a picture and modify it using the steps discussed earlier. Save it to your hard disk.

   It's recommended that the image be 200 × 200 pixels in image size or less, 60KB in file size or less, brightly lit, and visually simple, as just described.

2. Sign in to Google Places and open your business's Google Places page for editing. Scroll down to the Photos area.

3. Click the **Add a Photo from Your Computer** radio button.

   An entry area appears, along with a Browse button, and another button: Add Photo.

4. Click the **Browse** button.

   A dialog box appears enabling you to navigate to where the photo is stored on your hard disk.

5. Navigate to the photo and click **Open**.

   The text entry area fills in with the file pathway of the image you selected.

6. Click **Add Photo**.

   The photo is added to your Google Places editing window, and the number of photos uploaded is increased by one, as shown in Figure 7.3.

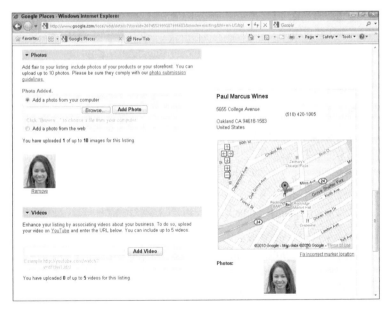

FIGURE 7.3   Thumbnail versions of photos you add show up in the Google Places editing window.

7. Add additional photos from your computer, using steps 1–6, or from the Web, using the steps in the next section.

The additional photos are added to your Google Places editing window, and the number of photos uploaded is increased by one for each.

8. Click **Submit**.

The photos are added to the Google Places listing for your business.

Adding a Picture from Picasa Web Albums

It's just as easy to add a photo to the Google Places page for your business from Picasa web albums as from your computer. Just follow these steps:

1. Take a picture and modify it using the steps shown earlier. Save it to your Picasa web album.

It's recommended that the image be 200 × 200 pixels in image size or less, 60KB in file size or less, brightly lit, and visually simple, as described earlier.

2. Sign in to Google Places and open your business's Google Places page for editing. Scroll down to the Photos area.

3. Click the **Add a Photo from the Web** radio button.

An entry area appears for the URL of the image, along with an Add Photo button.

4. Open a new browser window or tab and navigate to Picasa Web Albums. Log in, identify the photo you want to add, right-click on it to bring up the context-sensitive menu, and then choose the **Copy Shortcut** option, as shown in Figure 7.4.

The image URL is copied to your computer's Clipboard.

FIGURE 7.4   It's easy to grab pictures from Picasa web albums.

5. Return to the browser window or tab with your business's Google Places page open for editing. Paste the URL into the text entry field.

   The text entry area fills in with the URL.

6. Click **Add Photo**.

   The photo is added to your Google Places editing window, and the number of photos uploaded is increased by one, just as in the previous set of steps.

7. Add additional photos from Picasa, using steps 1–6 just discussed, or from your computer, using the steps in the previous section.

   The additional photos are added to your Google Places editing window, and the number of photos uploaded is increased by one for each photo you add.

8. Click **Submit**.

The photos are added to the Google Places listing for your business.

Removing a Photo from Your Page

Removing a photo is easy, and works the same wherever you've added it from. Follow these steps:

1. Return to the editing window for your business. Scroll down to the Photos area.

The photos you have added appear with a link, Remove, under each one, as shown in Figure 7.4.

2. Click the **Remove** link under the photo you want to remove.

The words *Photo Removed* appear in the Photos area.

3. Click **Submit**.

The photo is removed from your Google Places page.

Summary

In this lesson, you learned how photos enhance your Google Places page, how to take suitable photos, how to process photos on your computer for use online, how to follow Google Places rules for photos, how to add pictures to your Google Places page from your computer or Picasa web albums, and how to delete photos.

Adding Videos

In this lesson, you learn how videos help bring your Google Places page to life. You learned tips about how to take suitable videos, how to process videos on your computer for use online, how to follow the rules for videos on YouTube, how to add videos to your Google Places page from YouTube or elsewhere, and how to delete videos.

Adding Videos to Your Places Page

The Internet is increasingly becoming a distribution medium for video. From the Facetime feature on the iPhone 4, which allows live video phone calls, to ever-growing amounts of existing and new video made available online, web users spend more and more of their time watching video.

Google Places makes it easy to add up to five video clips to your Google Places listing. This is a big opportunity for your business to start using video.

However, it's an opportunity, not a requirement. It's very important to add photos to your Places page from the beginning or close to it. It's less necessary to move quickly to add video to your site.

You might be wondering just what video does to enhance a Google Places page—or a local business website, for that matter. The specifics of the answer are different for every business, but here are some potential benefits to consider:

▶ **Brings you and your people to life:** A video clip has the same kind of effect as a photograph, but more powerfully. It enables people to see the personality of whoever's in the video, which is likely to reassure them and make them more likely to want to do business with you.

▶ **Conveys information:** Many businesses have products or services that depend on technical-type information. For instance, if you have a grocery store, an occasional video clip showing how to cook a meal with this week's special foods is a real plus.

▶ **Shows off your skill:** Any decently produced video on your Google Places page or website shows that you are generally capable, willing to spend time and money to share what you do with people. Just like a nicely done display in a store, video can make a good impression.

TIP: **Don't Be Afraid to Borrow Videos**

You don't have to be all alone when it comes to videos—you can point to videos made by others that relate to products you carry, services you provide, big customers, and much more. You don't need permission for videos you only link to. These videos complement videos you make yourself, showing your staff, your store, your promotions, and your customers.

There are also some potential negatives to video. Here are some of the big concerns (and how to address them):

▶ **It's expensive:** Much web video is increasingly made cheaply and quickly. If you or a knowledgeable friend can get a few basics right (see the next section), you might be able to do it yourself, for little money.

▶ **It's lousy:** People often compare themselves to movie stars and their video clips to Hollywood movies. But people already come to see you all the time in your business; video just extends that. As long as the quality of your clip isn't insultingly bad, it will be an asset.

▶ **It's not seen:** Only a fraction of the people who visit your Google Places page will click on a video to start it, and only some of the ones who do will watch it to the end. Promote your video clips on your website and in person, and keep your investment low—of time and money both—so the cost/benefit ratio of using video is worthwhile.

> **CAUTION: Consider Model Releases for Videos**
>
> People can be touchy about having their image used. Consider getting model release forms, appropriate to your local area, for anyone you put in a video.

Your video clips don't have to be yours, or of you, to help your site. I made a video in 2008 (see Figure 8.1). Although politics can be divisive, the video does show me focused and energized. Also, the production quality of the video is high, which is a good, if indirect, reflection on me. I've used this video to help get consulting work; you might look for similar types of videos including you or your staff—or even simply on a relevant topic—to put on your Google Places page.

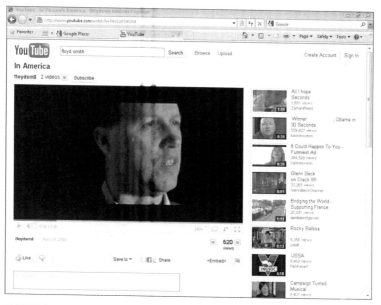

FIGURE 8.1   The author helped make a video in 2008.

Making Good Video Clips

Video powerfully engages people's minds and emotions. Because it affects us so much, what makes a good video is very hard to define. A grainy shot of a skateboarding dog might get millions of hits, whereas a professionally produced video introducing a new product might get very few.

Although it's hard to know just what a good video is, a low-quality clip can make your business look bad. Here are some tips for taking good photos for use online:

▶ **Get light on the subject:** People looking at a photo can stare at it. On video, with things moving around, light is even more important. Make sure the subject is well lit, as in the video shown in Figure 8.2.

FIGURE 8.2   The faces of subjects in this video got all the light.

▶ **Keep the light behind you:** As with photos, the brightest source of light should be behind the videographer, illuminating the faces of the subjects.

▶ **Go close, but off-center:** Close-ups are good in video, but not as tight a close-up as you might use in a photo. Leave some space around any "talking heads," and consider having the person's face slightly away from the center of the video image.

▶ **Choose your resolution:** To avoid annoying users, consider shooting your video in standard resolution at a 4:3 aspect ratio. Render such files at 640×480 resolution, which fills some, but not all, of the screen. Other choices are standard resolution, 16:9 aspect ratio, and rendering at 720×480 (this takes over nearly the entire screen), as well as high resolution, 16:9 aspect ratio, rendered at 1280×720 (this also takes over just about the entire screen).

▶ **Keep it brief:** In some experiments with online video usage by employees at a major bank, I found that many videos were watched for only 1 to 2 minutes. Consider making videos of this brief length for most purposes, and save longer ones for detailed demonstrations or recordings of events like a talk. (Even then, consider doing a brief highlights version of the longer video.)

▶ **Vary the old and the new:** Video is more expensive than photos, so plan to keep at least some videos around for a long time. A cooking demonstration can be used and reused for years, whereas this week's specials have to be introduced anew each, well, week.

▶ **Build up assets gradually:** You don't have to make your videos all at once. If you make one good video a quarter and add it to your site, you'll be way ahead of most potential competitors in no time.

▶ **Borrow, borrow, borrow:** If you like someone else's video clip and it's relevant to your business, shows you in a good light, or is otherwise a good fit, get whatever permissions are needed to show the video on your Google Places page or your website.

Unlike with photos, the impact of Photoshop and similar programs is not nearly as great. Even a brief video clip is made up of hundreds or thousands of separate images, and processing them all to, say, brighten them, is a major task. You can use programs like Adobe Premiere to help, but it's important to get the video you shoot to be as strong as possible before you

TIP: **Get Help with Video**

Find friends or colleagues who've made cool videos and ask them for help. A skilled amateur with a good idea and an hour or two to spare can easily produce something you, and your customers, will really like.

Video-Hosting Options

When you add photos to your Google Places page, as described in Lesson 7, "Adding Photos," you actually upload the photos to Google Places. Google stores them on its servers, and serves them up whenever the page is displayed. You're allowed 10 photos, of up to 1MB each, so that's only 10MB of "stuff"—and most people will, sensibly, use far less.

Video files, however, are much larger, and there are complex tradeoffs involved in uploading them, storing them, compressing them, and so on. Uncompressed, or lightly compressed, video files can take up many megabytes of disk storage, and download bandwidth, for every minute of video.

For this reason, Google Places doesn't allow you to upload video directly to the site, and it doesn't store video. Instead, it's up to you to get the video hosted someplace else, and then to get the web address, or URL, of the video. You paste that URL into Google Places to play the video.

TIP: **Get That URL**

To find the URL for a video that's already online, first check whether the site offers a URL for its videos; this is both convenient and implicit permission to use the video on your site. For videos where a URL is not displayed, choose **View**, **Source** or a similar option in your browser to view the HTML source code for the page, and then look for the video's URL. Check the copyright terms of the site before using the video. (Videos made by the U.S. government, for instance, are generally considered free to reuse.)

The leading website for hosting videos is YouTube, the wildly popular video-sharing site purchased by Google several years ago. YouTube has it all:

- Easy uploads

- Free compression

- Free storage

- Free bandwidth

- Publishes URL for reuse of videos

- Videos up to 10 minutes long supported

- Easy to create your own online "channel" for your videos

Most people can learn the basics of using YouTube by experimentation and by using the Help link that appears on the bottom of every page of YouTube. For more in-depth help appropriate to using videos for your business, consider books such as *Sams Teach Yourself YouTube in 10 Minutes* (Michael Miller, 2009).

YouTube is great for use as a hosting site for one or two videos. However, you can also really go to town and create a YouTube channel hosting your videos. This kind of effort is easily in the reach of local businesses. For instance, the San Francisco-based plumbing business Magic Plumbing has created a channel on YouTube, as shown in Figure 8.3.

> TIP: **Use Additional Details**
>
> If you create an online asset such as a YouTube channel, or a page on your website with more videos than are hosted on your Google Places page, you can use the Additional Details area of your page to point to the asset. Just create a suitable label and data for it, such as More Videos: www.youtube.com/user/magicplumbing.

> CAUTION: **Watch Out for Quality**
>
> YouTube compresses videos when you upload them in a way that can damage the image quality and the smoothness of video playback. If the quality of your video is important to you, compare YouTube to other available hosts, and learn whether there are ways to make your video look better online before proceeding.

FIGURE 8.3 YouTube channels can be your video home.

An increasingly popular alternative for hosting videos is Vimeo, shown in Figure 8.4, an upstart that positions itself as the main alternative to YouTube for video hosting. Vimeo's main emphasis is higher-quality video. Vimeo doesn't enforce a strict time limit on videos, but there are restrictions on the total amount of data you can upload and on the commercial use of videos you host there. Check out the site's options, and restrictions, carefully before deciding whether to host some or all of your videos on Vimeo.

YouTube and Vimeo aren't the only options. It's actually possible to link to just about any video on the Web and make it appear to be part of your Google Places page.

To get the URL for a video, open the web page with the video, and then choose **View**, **Source**, or a similar command, in your web browser. In the HTML code that appears, look for the URL of the video file. You can test this by putting the URL into the address area of a web browser. If the video, and only the video, appears on the page, you have the right URL.

FIGURE 8.4 Vimeo's high-quality videos are increasingly popular.

Unfortunately, there are likely to be intellectual property issues with using videos hosted on other sites, as well as the fact that the other site is paying hosting and downloading fees for the videos. Videos on YouTube and Vimeo are considered to be more or less fair game, but other videos might or might not be intended for sharing. When in doubt, contact the owner of a website for permission to use the video hosted there.

Following the Rules

The easiest, least restrictive, and recommend hosting site for videos linked to from Google Places is YouTube. Here are some of YouTube's rules for videos:

▶ **Use the right file type:** YouTube handles a wide variety of video file types. When in doubt, try uploading the file to YouTube as a test. If you use the common file types MOV, MP4, or 3gpp, you should flatten the video first. ("Flattening" is an option in most video editing programs that allows the video to be uploaded all in one piece.)

▶ **10-minute limit:** The biggest limitation on YouTube is the limit on the length of a video: 10 minutes. This shouldn't be a big problem for most videos you would want to include in a Google Places page. If 10 minutes is too short for you, though, consider Vimeo.

▶ **2GB limit:** The largest file size you can upload to YouTube is 2GB, which takes several hours to upload over a moderately fast connection. You'll probably never need anything like this kind of file size; even a lightly compressed video should only be a few megabytes in size per minute of playback length. With a 10-minute limit, it will be surprising if your file is more than 100MB, about 1/20th of the limit.

▶ **Policies:** YouTube videos have similar restrictions to photos and text content posted to your Google Places site: They can't violate privacy, contain threats or hate speech, and so on. For details, visit http://www.google.com/support/youtube/bin/answer.py?hl=en&answer=178909, as shown in Figure 8.5.

Adding a Video from YouTube

Google Places makes it quite easy to add a video from YouTube or any other hosting service. With a little more work—that is, digging up the URL, as described earlier in this lesson—you can actually add just about any video from the Web.

Follow these steps to host a video on your Google Places page:

1. Create a video clip and upload it to an online service such as YouTube. Alternatively, find a video online.

2. Sign in to Google Places and open your business's Google Places page for editing. Scroll down to the Videos area.

3. Open a new browser window or tab and navigate to YouTube, Vimeo, or other site hosting the video you want to use.

FIGURE 8.5 Follow YouTube policies to avoid causing yourself (and your customers) angst.

4. For YouTube, click the **Embed** button to display the URL. Set any other available options, such as a border and the video size. Then copy the URL from where it's displayed onscreen, as shown in Figure 8.6. For other hosting services such as Vimeo, select and copy the URL from where it's displayed onscreen. For videos on other sites, use the **View**, **Source** command to find the URL of the video. Put the URL in the address bar of another browser window or tab to test it.

5. Return to the browser window or tab with your business's Google Places page open for editing. Paste the URL into the text entry field.

   The text entry area fills in with the URL.

6. Click **Add Video**.

   The video is added to your Google Places editing window, and the number of videos uploaded is increased by one.

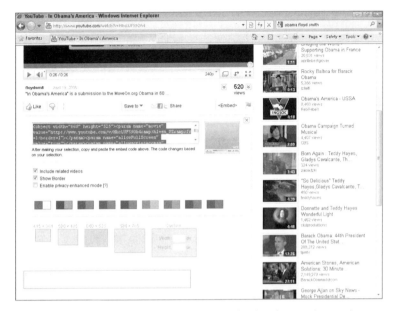

FIGURE 8.6   Get your URL from YouTube or other hosting service or site.

7. Add additional videos, using steps 1–6 just discussed.

> The additional videos are added to your Google Places editing window, and the number of videos uploaded is increased by one for each video URL you add.

8. Click **Submit**.

The videos are added to the Google Places listing for your business.

Removing a Video from Your Page

Removing a video is easy, and works the same wherever you've added it from. Follow these steps:

1. Return to the editing window for your business. Scroll down to the Videos area.

> The videos you have added appear with a link, Remove, under each one.

2. Click the **Remove** link under the video you want to remove.

The words *Video removed* appear in the Videos area.

3. Click **Submit**.

The photo is removed from your Google Places page.

Summary

In this lesson, you learned how videos help bring your Google Places page to life. You learned tips about how to take suitable videos, how to process videos on your computer for use online, how to follow the rules for videos on YouTube, how to add videos to your Google Places page from YouTube or elsewhere, and how to delete videos.

Adding Coupons

In this lesson, you learn how coupons can help your business. You then learn the specific elements that make up a coupon offer, and how to create versions of your coupon for display on the computer screen, on a mobile phone screen, and for printing. You then get to review the guidelines that Google Places offers for your coupon.

Building Your Business with Coupons

Google Insights says that online searches for coupons more than doubled in 2009. People are starting to understand that coupons can be part of an online offer and are starting to look for them. Google Places coupons give you an opportunity to be part of the action.

It's long been said that the most powerful words in marketing are *new* and *free*. Coupons are a quick way to put those powerful words to use for your business. The offer on the coupon is *new*—and, in most cases, time limited, creating urgency. And the coupon can either have a free offer, such as a free inspection or assessment, or a discount, which is free money compared to paying full price. See Figure 9.1 for an example of an online coupon.

In addition to the usual benefits of coupons, there is a strong additional reason for using Google Places coupons. You have the opportunity to create a habit with customers who find you on Google Places. You can associate your physical, local business with their Internet use. That way, the customers think of you whether they're shopping locally or online.

Customers who interact with your listing through a coupon might thereby be encouraged to take further actions, such as writing a review or sharing the listing with friends.

FIGURE 9.1   Online coupons can bring in business.

You also get the advantage of doing something new. Your potential customers have probably not had a lot of opportunity to use online coupons with local businesses. By offering an online coupon, you'll stand out.

TIP: **Coupons Are Good for Search Results**

Google Search likes coupons. As of this writing, having a coupon as part of your Google Places page increases the likelihood that it will place highly in search results. See Lesson 14, "Improving Search Engine Results," for details.

A coupon isn't worth much unless it causes the person who receives it to take action. There can be extra difficulty in getting someone to go from online to offline. Online sites have an advantage here because they can allow the person to complete a transaction while still online.

So, for all of these reasons, including the need for a mode switch from online to offline, you should make your coupon and the offer on it as compelling as possible. Find out what it really takes to get people to call, visit, and buy.

TIP: **Make Early Offers Irresistible**

Consider creating a super-compelling offer, such as a free hamburger from your hamburger stand, just to see how many people bite (no pun intended). Such an offer might even pay for itself in add-on sales of drinks and fries, as well as multiperson parties visiting with just one or two coupons in hand. If you are indeed losing a bit of money on the offer, decide in advance how many people can take advantage of it before you change the offer. Then, when the redemptions take too big a chunk out of profits, make the change.

Getting Clicks

Each of your coupons has four parts:

- **An advertisement:** The advertisement appears next to search results. This is just two lines. The first line, the headline (up to 25 characters), shows up highlighted as a clickable link; the second line, the subheading (up to 35 characters), is nonactive text beneath it. You don't get anywhere with your coupon unless the user clicks on the link.

- **The online summary:** This is what the users see on the Google Maps listing when they click on the link. The summary has only the advertisement plus details, up to 250 characters (about 40 words, although you shouldn't use that many). These details have to attract the user to view the printed coupon.

- **The printed coupon:** The printed coupon adds a picture and an expiration date, if you include them in the coupon setup. The whole package has to inspire the user to either print out the coupon and bring it in, or, optionally, show it on a mobile phone at your business.

- **The mobile coupon:** This is a mobile version of your coupon that highlights the expiration date, hopefully reminding the user to get on into your business before the coupon expires.

You can put in endless hours on each of these parts, and there are experts who will do this for you as well. However, assuming you're more or less a beginner—with online coupons, if not with printed ones—I focus here on the advertisement part. This is the toughest nut to crack.

NOTE: **Online Coupons and AdWords Work Together**
The skills you develop for creating and managing online coupons
are also very useful with Google AdWords, a powerful tool for building up local businesses. See Lesson 11, "Advertising with Tags and
AdWords," for details.

Before you even start writing your advertisement, a lot of work has already
been done for you. The users know that the ad is probably local and relevant because they're doing local search on something they care about.
They'll have been exposed to Google ads many times before, and probably
clicked on a few—enough to form an opinion as to their usefulness. If that
opinion is a positive one (and it probably is because Google's ad business
grows by billions of dollars every year), the users are ready to click if they
see a good offer.

The advertisement consists of just two lines of text:

▸ **The headline is just 25 characters long:** It's displayed as a
  clickable link leading to the online summary (which repeats the
  advertisement and adds the details field).

▸ **The subheading is only 35 more characters:** The subheading is
  optional, but almost everyone uses it. The subheading gives you a
  chance to add a bit of depth, detail, even humor, to the headline.

The advertisement has to do two things: offer people something desirable, and reassure them that the offer will work for them. Although there
are many, many ways to use the two lines available to you, typically, you
put the offer in the first, clickable line and the reassuring details in the
second line.

The headline can be only 25 characters long (about 5 words)! Here are
some examples of possible offers to fit in this small typographical budget:

▸ **A discount:** A percentage discount from normal pricing. A discount of 10% is commonly used; anything greater than 20%
  might arouse suspicion as to the value of what you're offering,
  and your motives in getting the user to contact you.

▸ **A fixed price:** A fixed price for a product or service. The Google
  example shows a two-topping pizza for $10. People want to

know in advance what they're going to pay. (It's embarrassing to walk out of a store empty-handed, or out of a restaurant with an empty stomach, because the prices were too high.) By offering a fixed price, you limit the customer's risk in investigating and making the purchase to that fixed amount.

▶ **Free initial consultation (also free inspection, examination, assessment, and so forth)**: Free brake inspection, free pest check, and first session free, as shown in Figure 9.1, are all examples of this kind of offer. A free initial meeting and offering of service gives you the chance to engage with your customer, making a strong (and hopefully positive) impression.

Offering a free initial assessment risks shifting in favor of the customer—giving the potential customer something valuable to you up front, in the hopes that it leads to paying business.

▶ **Free reports (also brochures, listings, white papers, and so on)**: Best if locally relevant: recent home sales in Rockridge or new business trends in Oakland, for instance. Offering free information enables you to give value to customers at very little per-unit cost to yourself. The customers also have low costs because they have to spend time with the free information only if they are finding it valuable as they go along. Risk is low on both sides, but so is the level of engagement between you and the customer.

The headline is the main driver of clicks for your coupon, and therefore of possible redemptions. Be prepared to try different headline options and see which ones get the highest percentage of clickthroughs.

The subheading's job is to add details that reassure the users that it's worth their time and effort to click on the heading. The details given should be predictable ones; the surprise should be in the offer.

The subheading can be only 35 characters (about 7 words), and you probably want even fewer. Here are some examples of details that you can usefully include in a subheading:

▶ **More about the offer itself**: Let customers know if there are conditions—but also that the offer isn't so restricted as to be useless. "Free delivery" reassures the users that they won't be dinged

by hidden costs; "Saturdays only" might be a good way for you
to shift business to a slower period.

▶ **More about the product or service:** People often need details to
make a decision. What type of restaurant is offering a discount?
("Thai-Indian fusion" might do it.) What are the qualifications of
the yoga teacher offering a fixed-price session? ("Trained in
India" might be a good statement to be able to make.)

▶ **Superlatives:** Anything you can credibly say about *best, fastest,
first, most helpful,* and so on will reassure customers that they're
dealing with a winner. Be ready to back up your claim, even if
it's only with research that you've done yourself.

The main point with advertisement text is to experiment! There are endless
possibilities for what might cause customers to click through, and what
works today might not work tomorrow. The only way for you to get to the
right answer is to try a lot of possibilities, assess the results, and then use
what you learn to try some more.

TIP: **Listen to Your Customers About Coupons**

Your past and current coupons, ads, offers, and website are great
sources of ideas for coupons—so are things customers tell you
that they like and dislike about your own business and the competition. After you get coupons up, listen carefully to what people tell
you about them so that you can use the information to improve
future offers.

Creating a Coupon

The great thing about Google Places coupons is how flexible they are. You
can create them, change them—the wording, the offer, the look—and with-
draw them at any time. So, there's no reason not to get started now.

NOTE: **It's Getting Better All the Time**

Even experts have to start somewhere. I once did an informal
study of corporate videos made at a top international bank. Almost

every executive who performed on video started out with very simple videos, often poorly lit, and with the executive talking at people rather than to them. The best performers were simply the executives who had gotten started early, and then kept at it often enough—and long enough—to get better. It can be the same for your videos, coupons, and so forth.

Follow these steps to create a Google Places coupon:

1. Go to http://www.google.com and sign in to the Google account associated with your business. Choose **Settings**, **Google Account Settings**. From the list of Google products that appears, choose **Google Places**.

   Your Google Places Dashboard opens.

2. Click the **Coupons** tab. Then click **Add a Coupon Now**.

   The Coupons page opens, as shown in Figure 9.2.

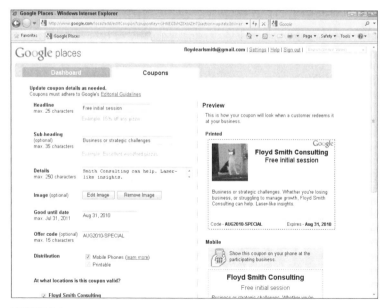

FIGURE 9.2   Coupons are pretty simple.

3. Enter the headline, up to 25 characters.

This text will be shown as a clickable link in the ad for your coupon and in the summary version on Google Maps, and will display in all versions of your coupon.

See the previous section for specific recommendations on what to put in the headline.

4. Enter the subheading, up to 35 characters.

The subheading will be shown as plain text in the ad for your coupon, and will display in all versions of your coupon.

NOTE: **How to Use Subheads?**

See the previous section, "Getting Clicks," for specific recommendations on what to put in the subheading.

---

5. Enter details, up to 250 characters.

The details will not be shown in the ad for your coupon, but will display in all versions of your coupon.

The details text is where you can add any terms and conditions (T&Cs) because the coupon needs to be complete in itself. You can also add business details. I recommend that you add just enough information about your business to support the offer and encourage someone to come in.

6. To add an image, click the **Add Image** button. Choose your computer, Picasa web albums, or a web address (URL) as the source. Follow the onscreen prompts to add the image, similar to the process described in Lesson 7, "Adding Photos."

The Upload a Picture dialog appears, as shown in Figure 9.3. When the image is added, it displays only in the printable coupon.

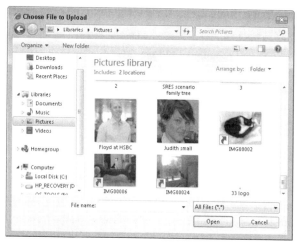

FIGURE 9.3   Upload a picture for your business.

TIP: **Keep It Sweet and Simple**

People are creatures of habit. Consider using an image for the printed version of your coupon that also appears on your Google Places page, your website, and in other marketing materials so that they have a single visual point of reference for your business.

You want to create a single iconic image for your business that ties to your name and place. If your business name is eponymous—named after founders or a family—then an image of one or two of these people probably works. If it's place based, the location or the owner standing in the business might work well.

The growth of online sites such as Facebook has only increased the importance of having iconic images for use online, plus other images in support. You can use something handy to get started, but consider hiring a professional to help create a single image that you can use and reuse.

7. Enter a Good Until date.

Enter a Good Until date, after which the offer expires. Decide how long you want the offer to last. Having an offer last a whole month gives you the opportunity to really test it without the offer seeming to be eternal (and therefore not motivating). At the end of the period, consider having another, different offer ready to replace it.

8. Enter an offer code.

The offer code (up to 15 characters) appears on only the printed and mobile versions of your coupon. An offer code is for you to use in tracking, if you're making so many offers that you need to manage them. The code is visually intrusive on the (printed and mobile) coupons, so you should use it only if you really need it; the coupon itself is pretty self-documenting for tracking purposes. (Although you might want to record the details of mobile coupons at the time of redemption because there is, literally, no paper trail.)

9. Click the check box to enable or disable a mobile phone version of the coupon.

Mobile phone versions of your coupon are great; they help your customers use their technological toys to bring you new business. They're harder to track than paper coupons, but for most businesses, it should be worth a bit of extra effort to do so.

10. For each of your locations, click the check box to enable or disable the coupon for that location.

This option means that the coupon will be shown only for searches that turn up one of the locations for which the location check box is checked. You can use this option to make an offer in only some locations or to make different offers at different locations.

TIP: **Accept Coupons if Possible**

You will need to prepare your people for what to do if a coupon (printed or mobile) is presented at a location where it's not meant to be valid. "Gracefully accept it," if at all possible, is my recommendation.

11. Review the results of your entries so far, and then click **Continue**.

The coupon is created and saved. It displays in a list of all your current coupons, as shown in Figure 9.4.

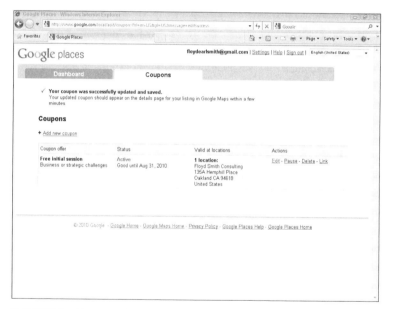

FIGURE 9.4   You get a list of coupons to edit.

CAUTION: **Tracking Offer Codes Can Be Hard**

The offer code doesn't display in your list of coupons, so it's thereby more difficult to separate similar offers from each other in the list.

Checking Coupon Guidelines

Google Places has a long set of guidelines for coupons, ranging from practical advice to musts that apply specifically to coupons.

Here are some highlights:

► **You say it, you own it:** The offer you're making must be legal, and you must be able to fulfill it.

► **Use plain English:** Avoid excessive use of CAPITAL LETTERS, strange <<<punctuation>>>, and so on. Spelling and grammar should be correct. Avoid repetition, as in phrases such as *sale sale sale*.

► **Make restrictions clear:** "One per customer" and similar restrictions must be made crystal clear and enforced (somehow) by you because there's no way to limit the number of times an offer can be printed, or displayed from a mobile phone screen, by a given customer.

► **Make the offer special:** The offer should be available through only the coupon and similar coupons in other media (for example, a coupon in a circular or newspaper). Coupons should not repeat normal standing offers, such as "20% off Tuesdays," offered to all customers.

To see the up-to-date specifics, visit the official Google page, shown in Figure 9.5: http://www.google.com/support/places/bin/answer.py?hl=en&answer=48187.

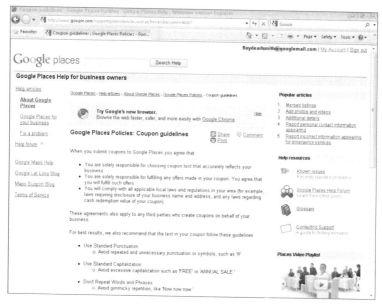

FIGURE 9.5 Check the guidelines before you create and publish your coupon.

Summary

In this lesson, you learned how coupons can help your business. You then learned the elements that make up a coupon offer, and how to create versions of your coupon for display on the computer screen, on a mobile phone screen, and for printing. You then learned about the guidelines that Google Places offers for your coupon.

Posting Real-Time Updates

In this lesson, you learn how real-time updates can bring new life to your Google Places page (and your business). You learn about the types of real-time updates that might make sense for your business, such as updates to business hours and special offers; how to post and delete updates; how to enter and shorten URLs; and how to use Twitter in conjunction with real-time updates.

Using Real-Time Updates

A real-time update—Google also calls the feature "post to your Place page"—is a brief text that brings an element of life to your page. The posting is up to 160 characters long, the same length as a Twitter tweet. The maximum of 160 characters is only the upper limit; most tweets are much shorter.

So, how does anyone communicate successfully with such a limited amount of space? Mostly by taking advantage of context. It's potentially funny for Paris Hilton to tweet, "Just had another blonde moment"; for Scarlett Johansson to tweet the same thing wouldn't make much sense (unless she were referring to Paris Hilton).

You can do the same thing with your business. Your Google Places page visitors know, at the least, the name of your business, the type of business you're in, and where you're located. If they've visited your business, they know much more. So, your real-time updates can take advantage of this shared knowledge to communicate a lot in 160 characters or even fewer.

NOTE: **Use Google Places with Twitter**

Google Places real-time updates are worth using on their own, but they become much more powerful when used in combination with a Twitter account. See the section on Twitter later in this lesson to learn more about using them together.

Figure 10.1 shows a real-time update on the Floyd Smith Consulting Places page. Google Places shows only one update at a time. You can work around this by linking to your Twitter feed, if you have one. It's also a good way to get more followers on Twitter.

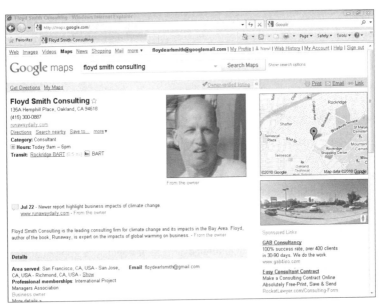

FIGURE 10.1   Real-time updates go right in the middle of your Google Places page.

The purpose, and best use, of real-time updates might be a bit hard to grasp. From a big-picture point of view, having these updates brings life to your Google Places page. It gives people a reason to keep coming back to your page, and helps you get the latest information to people who visit the page.

Here are some ideas for getting the most out of real-time updates:

▶ **Post daily:** Consider creating a fresh post every day. This keeps your Google Places page lively and makes sure that you are always thinking of the best way to use the position that the real-time update occupies on your Google Places page.

▶ **Include web links:** Just type in a web address within your real-time update; Google Places will display it as a clickable link. By including web links in your real-time updates, you can increase traffic to your site, helping to boost your site's search engine ranking.

▶ **Link to your posts on your website:** Consider keeping a record of all your posts on your website and linking to it from your Google Places page (or, if you have one, link to your Twitter account). You can include the link in each real-time update (perhaps using a URL shortener; see later in this lesson), or put it in the Additional Details area, described in Lesson 6, "Improving Your Google Places Page."

The main types of updates are changes to opening hours, special offers, events, new products and services, updates, relevant news, and random thoughts. Each type of update can have a specific purpose for contributing to your business. Descriptions of each type follow.

NOTE: **Manage Your "Online Billboard"**

Your Google Places page displays only one real-time update at a time, but that update is posted pretty prominently. So, think of the real-time update position as a kind of online billboard. Keep it filled with interesting, useful, relevant, and appealing information that's likely to help customers and bring them into your store or to get them to call you.

Changes to Opening Hours

If you never use real-time updates to your Google Places page for anything else, use them for changes to opening hours. Your Google Places page (and your website) should always feature any changes in your opening hours, and clearly state your holiday hours as well (even if they're unchanged from normal hours).

TIP: **Let People Know When You're Open**

In addition to your Google Places page, use your answering machine message to keep people updated on your regular business hours, changes to your opening hours, and holiday hours. I rarely encounter a small business that takes this obvious and important step, so you'll stand out, in a good way, if you do.

Here are some examples: "We'll be open during our normal hours, 9 a.m. to 5 p.m., on President's Day, Monday, February 21st." As someone running your own business, you might not realize just how many holidays there are, many of which are observed by schools, banks, state offices, and so on. Figure 10.2 shows part of a list of holidays for the United States; note that this doesn't include state holidays.

Other holidays are just celebrations, without an officially sanctioned day off, but still a possible marketing opportunity for you to tie into. Cinco de Mayo, Columbus Day, and St. Patrick's Day are examples.

The whole advantage to your customers of your being present as a local business is that you thereby make it convenient for them to do business with you. If your opening hours are not what your customers expect, that convenience is significantly eroded. It probably doesn't take very many disappointments—for the customer to expect, or hope, that you're open, and then find out that you're not—to significantly reduce a customer's chances of doing business with you.

Posting changes to your opening hours gets several things done at once:

▶ Gives you a chance to reduce frustration when you close during normal business hours

FIGURE 10.2 U.S. federal holidays.

▶ Gives you a chance to increase business when you're open extra hours

▶ Gives you a chance to increase business when you're open on a holiday, when people might otherwise not try you because they expect that you're off for the holiday

> TIP: **Use Holidays to Build Your Business**
>
> For some customers, the best opportunity for them to visit your business, perhaps for the first time ever, is when they have the day off work for a holiday—and you stay open. Use Google Places page and other marketing tools to reassure people that you are indeed open, and consider having a special event such as a sale.

Always, always, always post a real-time update when your hours are different than usual, as well as to clarify the situation with regard to your opening hours on and around holidays. This will teach people to use your Google Places page—or your website, if you post the updates there as well—as a handy place to find out what they can expect.

Specials

For many businesses, advertising specials is the meat and potatoes of real-time updates. Because your use of Google Places, and the online world in general, is probably fairly new to your business, and therefore to your customers, you should use real-time updates of online specials in several different ways:

▶ To extend real-world marketing campaigns that appear in your store, in advertisements, and so on to your Google Places page

▶ To tie into online and print coupons

▶ To extend Twitter announcements of specials

▶ To create specials only announced in real-time updates, testing the effectiveness of real-time updates and your Google Places page

The best way to get people to keep doing something is to give them a reward for doing it. So, you should always have a special of some sort on your Google Places page, even if that's the only place the special appears, unless you have some other, relatively urgent posting.

Here are some examples of specials:

▶ "Call now for a 10% discount on your next purchase." Variations: "...your next purchase of more than $20" or "...your next purchase of less than $20."

▶ "Come into today, and mention this ad, for a free apple" or "test drive," or "marketing evaluation," or anything else that's relevant to your business.

▶ "Get four for the price of three on all products, this week only."

▶ "Visit our website for a special free offer. http://www.runawaydaily. com/special."

> TIP: **Give Complete Information in Updates**
>
> Make your updates complete. Give relevant opening hours, provide web links, and do anything else needed to help customers act on the offers and information you provide.

Events

Business today is all about being close to your customers. Businesses use expensive software, or online services such as the website salesforce.com, to know more about their prospects, customers, and former customers.

As a local business, you are, literally, close to your customers. That's the good news. The bad news is that the number of people who will come visit you—your "catchment area," as the Brits put it—is limited.

So, you need to get as high a percentage of people who are physically nearby to come and do business with you as possible. Events are a great way to do this. You can have speakers, demos, tastings, and more, depending on the type of business you own.

Your Google Places page is one good place to publicize events. Examples include the following:

▶ "This Friday, 6–9 p.m.: Extra hours and conversation with the owner, Thelma Johnson."

▶ "All day Saturday: Clown time! Come in for free face painting, balloon twisting, and magic, plus all our great products and services."

▶ "Monday morning blues? We've doubled our usual staff and halved our prices for a pre-inventory clear-out, from 9 a.m.–1 p.m. Monday."

> CAUTION: **Pay Attention to Marketing**
>
> If you spend time, effort, and money on an event, don't undermarket it. In these cases, Google Places shouldn't be your only marketing, but just one part of a larger effort to make sure that your business is packed with people from beginning to end of your event.

New Products and Services

Like events, new products and services should be widely publicized. Use your Google Places page to help get the word out.

Unlike events, though, new products and services aren't necessarily expensive to bring in; they're a normal part of doing business. So, you can publicize them as broadly or narrowly as you care to. Because Google Places real-time updates are cheap and easy, you can use them for both minor and major announcements.

In some cases, Google Places real-time updates might be the only way you publicize new products and services. You can even publicize the arrival of new shipments of a product with a real-time update—and use a special offer to help identify fans of that product for future marketing efforts.

Here are a few examples:

▶ "New service: New Year's sales planning! Call us now at 510-555-1212 to plan for next year."

▶ "New product: Cucinatori tomato ketchup from Italy! Half off this week, if you come in and mention this ad."

▶ "New shipment of Mercury scarves just in! Announced here first! Come in now to see and buy the scarves with the best patterns and colors."

News, Opinion, and Desiderata

News is a really flexible topic area. You can keep your news updates hyper-local, just posting about what happens with the business. Or you can post more broadly, posting about things that affect your local area or the industry your business is part of.

CAUTION: **Use Updates Sparingly**

Don't post general news via real-time updates to your Google Places page. People have lots of sources for news today, especially online, and it will just confuse them if you add your Google Places page to the list of sources from which they get general news. Keep your updates to news relevant to your specific business.

You can post on some or all of the following:

- ▶ **Personnel changes or comings and goings:** "Come say hi to our new counterperson, Mickey Finn."

- ▶ **News about your business and results:** (Tip: Accentuate the positive.) "Record number of new customers added last month. Thank you, and keep coming in!"

- ▶ **Local construction or other changes that affect access to your business:** "The stoplight on our corner is out of commission again—be careful when you drive by!"

- ▶ **Changes in your business or product areas:** "Lean crop of tomatoes this season; buy purees, pasta sauces, and so on now, before prices rise."

You can also include opinion and desiderata—more or less random thoughts, which can be on relevant topics, or addressing "life, the universe, and everything," to borrow the title of a Douglas Adams book. Sarah Palin got a lot of attention a little while ago for a tweet in which she compared her travails with the English language to Shakespeare's.

This kind of thing doesn't work for most people, but it conveys personality and humor, which might lead people to come into your business. If you have a quirky personality, time on your hands, and want to try to be the first Google Places star via your real-time updates, go for it!

> TIP: **Prioritize the Good Stuff**
>
> The space used by the one and only real-time update that can be displayed on your Google Places page at a time is precious. Prioritize changes to opening hours, specials, and events over new products and services, news, and other information. Then use customer actions and feedback to determine what's really working for you.

Posting and Deleting Real-Time Updates

Real-time updates are pretty simple because they're text-only and are limited to 160 characters. (You can include a clickable web URL just by typing in the full URL; see the next section for details.) You just go to the right page, type in the update, and see it appear on your Google Places page a few minutes later.

> CAUTION: **Look Out for Misteaks**
>
> Be sure to spell-check and grammatically check your postings. Any misteaks (mistake intended) severely undermine the impression you want to make with potential customers; you're better off not posting at all than posting updates with errors. Consider getting others to look at the posting and check any web links, both before and shortly after you publish the listing, to make sure you've gotten rid of any errors.

You can easily delete a real-time update from the same page you entered it from.

Follow these steps to enter a real-time update:

1. Go to http://www.google.com and sign into the Google account associated with your business. Choose **Settings**, **Google Account Settings**. From the list of Google products that appears, choose **Google Places**.

   Your Google Places Dashboard opens.

2. For the site you want to update, click the business name.

   Your Google Places information page opens. The currently displayed real-time update, if any, is displayed in the upper-right corner, as shown in Figure 10.3.

3. To delete an existing real-time update, find it in the upper-right corner and click the **Delete** link next to it.

   The current entry is deleted. You can click the Sign Out link to exit your Google Places Dashboard or continue working.

4. In the area in the upper right, called **Post to Your Place Page**, enter your text.

   The counter just under the text entry box decrements as you enter each character to show the number of characters you have left to enter. The count starts from 160 and decreases.

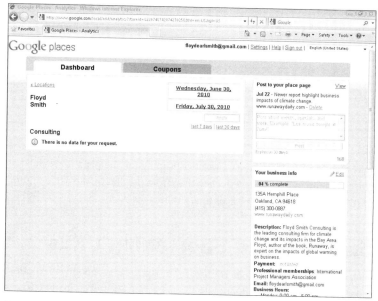

FIGURE 10.3   Enter your update, including web URLs, in the text entry box.

Although it's not required, I recommend that you spell-check your entry using a program such as Microsoft Word. You might also consider getting a friend or employee with good editing skills to take a look; many potentially embarrassing mistakes, such as using *it's* instead of *its*, aren't caught by most spell checkers.

5. To enter a clickable URL, enter the full URL.

If the URL begins with "www.", enter it as is; if it doesn't, add the characters "http://" to the front of the link so that Google Places recognizes it as a URL and displays it as a clickable link. Google Places will display the URL as a clickable link.

6. Click **Post** to post the update.

Your update appears on your Google Places page within a few minutes. You can click the Sign Out link to exit your Google Places Dashboard or continue working.

TIP: **Include Images in Your Updates**

You can use Twitter to fairly easily post links to images as part of your Google Places real-time update, as described later in this lesson. You can also post the image to your organization's web page, Flickr, or Picasa web albums, or some other service, and then include the URL in your posting. Optionally, you can also use a URL shortener (see the next section).

Now that your posting is up, check it carefully for errors and test any URLs in it (see next section). Consider printing out the page for review; editing from paper is more effective than from the screen. Also, having the posting on paper makes it easier to ask others for their input.

Entering and Shortening URLs

Including clickable URLs in your real-time updates is a good way to offer more information or an opportunity to take action. However, many URLs are very long. You can shorten a URL to something much more compact by using a URL-shortening service such as the website bit.ly. You can see bit.ly in operation in Figure 10.4.

NOTE: **Don't Expect Everyone to Click**

Research shows that every additional step you ask a user to take tends to sharply decrease the number of people who complete an action. So, although it's good to offer people clickable links, don't expect the majority of people to actually click them.

Like other URL-shortening services, bit.ly converts a long URL to a much shorter one. When you enter the URL, bit.ly stores it in a table, and returns to you a much shorter, computer-generated URL, beginning with the service's own web domain name, bit.ly.

When a user clicks the shorter, computer-generated URL, a request goes out to the web servers that host the bit.ly domain. The longer URL you entered is returned, and the user goes there instead.

Now there is something nice about full URLs. The users can see whether the website involved is one they know and trust, and can often tell a lot about the target page from the rest of the URL, as well. The chances that the user will click are probably higher if you use the full URL.

FIGURE 10.4   The web service bit.ly shortens URLs for you.

However, it's become kind of cool to use a URL shortener, partly because they're strongly associated with Twitter (see the next section), and partly because the use of a URL shortener shows that you're making an effort to keep your messages compact.

If your message, when including the full URL, is fewer than 160 characters, you have no choice but to use a URL-shortening service. If the full URL fits, you can use it, or use a shortened URL instead.

Using Real-Time Updates with Twitter

Twitter is a service that gets talked about a lot, but that's poorly understood by many. Twitter allows its users to create messages of up to 160 characters in length. The messages can include web URLs, and Twitter will upload and host photos and then put a URL to the photo in a message. Each message is called a *tweet*. Figure 10.5 shows the tweets from one not particularly famous Twitter user.

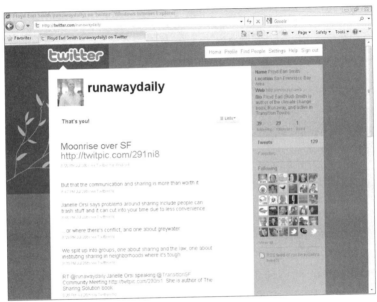

FIGURE 10.5   Twitter is a great complement to Google Places real-time updates.

NOTE: **Get Into Twitter Fast**

For an effective, whirlwind introduction to Twitter, see *Sams Teach Yourself Twitter in 10 Minutes* by Tee Morris (Sams, 2009).

Twitter's use of the words *Twitter* and *tweet*, somewhat whimsical when applied to computer-generated messages, has led to a lot of jokes, including Twitter users being referred to as *twits*. However, Twitter is serious; it has hundreds of millions of users, and billions of tweets have been sent.

Companies, activists, celebrities, and others use it to maintain contact with customers, followers, fans, and more. Many people who rarely, if ever, send a tweet use Twitter to stay up-to-date with relevant news. But many others—a majority of people—have no interest in or use for the service at all. Even if your customer is a Twitter user, but there's no guarantee that they'll follow your Twitter account, receiving your updates. So, you can accomplish a lot with Twitter, but you can't use it to reach all, or even most, of your customers.

If you have a Twitter account that you use for your business, or are willing to consider creating one and sending out regular tweets, Google Places real-time updates take on a whole new dimension.

Because Google Places real-time updates are exactly the same length as tweets, each of your tweets can potentially be copied and pasted, unchanged, as a Google Places real-time update. Just use the steps earlier in this lesson.

If you create a tweet with a link to a photo, the tweet—with the same link—will work just fine in Google Places.

You will probably want to tweet on Twitter more than you want to update your Google Places real-time updates. The kind of news and whimsical items that are of dubious value in the one and only real-time updates slot on the Google Places page work well on Twitter, where establishing a personality is so important.

However, this doesn't take away from the fact that Twitter and Google Places real-time updates can work very well together. Be ready to experiment, and enjoy yourself as you go along. Not only will that make the work easier, but your relaxed attitude will help make you a more effective Twitterer and real-time-updater.

Summary

In this lesson, you learned how real-time updates can bring new life to your Google Places page and your business. You learned about the types of real-time updates that might make sense for your business, such as updates to business hours and special offers. You learned how to post and delete updates, how to enter and shorten URLs, and how to use Twitter in conjunction with real-time updates.

LESSON 11

Advertising with Tags and AdWords

In this lesson, you learn how to use tags in Google Places and get a brief introduction to Google AdWords. You come to understand how advertising can help you and what tags are available in Google text search and Google Maps search for your Google Places page. You then see how Google AdWords can help you get more online traffic for your business.

The Value of Advertising

Local businesses, which are often on the smaller side, have long been big users of advertising. Local businesses are also likely to be good at *guerrilla marketing*—getting the word out at low or no cost. Google Places is in itself a guerrilla marketing tool, a very low-cost way to help people find you. It also offers QR codes (covered in Lesson 12, "Using the Dashboard") and tags, two additional tools for guerrilla marketing. And it ties into Google AdWords—which can range from very cheap to very expensive, depending on how you use it. The biggest question for small business is always whether advertising is effective. It all goes back to the famous quote by department store magnate John Wanamaker, shown in Figure 11.1: "Half the money I spend on advertising is wasted; the trouble is, I don't know which half."

Although "free" is a good price, there are only so many hours in a day. Much of the benefit of Google Places can be had for little or no expenditure of money, but it all takes time. So, even for free options, you need to know what's effective and what isn't. Much of the potential value of all your Google Places advertising depends on the positioning you choose. For any innovation, you and your business can take on a position of

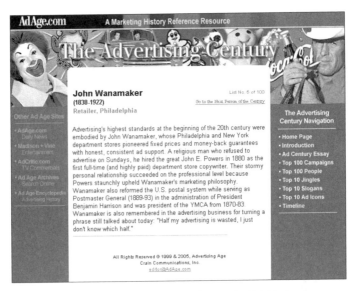

FIGURE 11.1   John Wanamaker was sure he was half right about advertising.

aggressively adopting it, ignoring it, or something in-between. Google Places is no exception. Your choice of how aggressively to use a new tool such as Google Places is a risk-reward tradeoff. Being a leader has a high risk of wasting your time and money if the innovation doesn't take off or if you use it poorly. But being a leader also has a high possibility of reward if the new technique or tool works and you're seen as effective in using it. Relating to Google Places, or most other innovations, possible positions include the following:

▶ **Leader:** You jump on the bandwagon early and push your lead hard, taking advantage of most of the new features and functions to get new business. People recognize you as being out in front. Leadership positions with successful innovations can be built into a permanent competitive advantage.

▶ **Fast follower:** Let others you know go first and see how they fare. Then follow up quickly if they seem to be doing well, or if

they are flailing but you think you can do better. You are still rec-
ognized as being an early adopter, and, with hard work, you
might even be able to beat the leaders who got out there first.

▶ **Follower:** You go with the flow—let others go first, and proceed
when it starts to feel painful to be left out. You don't get much
praise, but you don't get much criticism either. Achieving leadership is unlikely.

▶ **Laggard:** You wait until nearly everyone around you has already
acted, and then get on board yourself—often at lower cost, and
with low risk, but also having missed any of the possible reward
from early action. You'll never be the leader. Some customers
and business colleagues will think that you're out of it or that you
missed the boat.

There's nothing wrong with taking any of these positions. In fact, it's rare
that any one business is a leader or a laggard in everything. Google Places
is a good opportunity to take a leadership or fast follower position, though,
because it's free or low cost to do so. Also, with Google's growing influence, it's probably something you'll have to do eventually. The only question is whether you'll do the work sooner or later. Getting involved sooner
is inconvenient, and you might spend more time by going now than if you
wait for others to learn their way around, to share knowledge, and for low-
cost support services to spring up. However, you won't spend that much
more time, especially with this book in your hand. And if you go ahead
now, you are highly likely to be a leader or fast follower. The advertising
capabilities described in this lesson—QR codes, tags for advertising, and
Google AdWords—are all still marks of a leadership approach to Google
Places, at least in most markets. Use them to get ahead, and stay ahead, of
the competition.

TIP: **Impress Your Customers**

Users will be impressed by tags the first time they see one (and
will continue to be impressed because they're relatively rare). So,
realize that there's some novelty value in being an early adopter of
tags, perhaps above and beyond the calculated financial return.

Using Different Types of Tags

A tag is a way of enhancing your listing. Just like the Yellow Pages sells features such as bold text, a box around your listing, an image, and so forth, Google sells tags (see Figure 11.2).

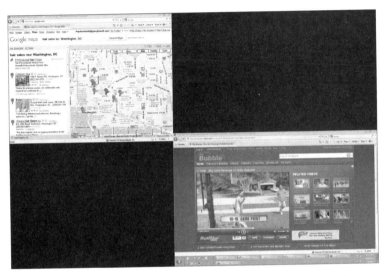

FIGURE 11.2   Tags jump out from search listings.

CAUTION: **Your Mileage May Vary**

Tags are being rolled out gradually by Google. They might not be available yet in your area. Google might or might not announce if or when tags will be available; so if they aren't, you have little choice but to wait and see whether they do become available.

CAUTION: **Pricing Not Fair to All Businesses**

The flat pricing for tags is a bit unfair because $25 a month is a lot more forbidding to some businesses than others. So, do your homework before deciding whether to use tags, and monitor their effectiveness carefully, as described in this lesson and the next one.

You can choose from just a short list of possibilities—with my suggestions as to the ones that could potentially be the most effective first:

▶ A link to a coupon for your business

▶ A link to a menu or reservations page

▶ A link to your business website

▶ A link to photos or videos of your business

▶ A link to posts for your business

The last tag shows when the post was updated. You get to choose a specific type of tag only if you already have that feature in your listing. For example, you can choose a coupon tag only if you've created a coupon, as described in Lesson 9, "Adding Coupons." The same is true for website links, photos, posts, and so on. All the tag types look like fun—but many of them require extra work to mean much. Also, users encounter tags when they're searching for specific information, so a tag either has to help meet their specific information need, be so interesting as to distract users from it, or both. Here's a bit of detail on each of the tag types and how you might use it:

▶ **Coupons:** Coupons should directly generate revenue—at a hit, of course, to profits—and tags help make coupons more effective. You can do a quick cost-benefit analysis to find out whether the coupon program, including the amount you spend on a tag for it, is paying off for you.

▶ **Menus and reservations pages:** For the right kind of business, such as restaurants, users can be assumed to be quite curious about what's on the menu, and making a reservation leads directly to business (assuming most users follow through). So, a tag for a menu or reservations page should be good for business.

▶ **A website link:** If your type of business seems highly web friendly or web enabled, users will be likely to follow a tag to your business website. However, your tag has to give users a reason to go to your site right then and there; otherwise, users might just mentally note that you have a website and go on.

▸ **A link to photos or videos:** Multimedia of this type is often seen as supportive or supplemental, so I'm not convinced that very many users will choose to link off to it in the midst of a search for specific information that isn't likely to directly involve photos or videos.

▸ **A link to a post:** The odds that the user is looking for something that your latest post was about (see Lesson 10, "Posting Real-Time Updates") are low, so this might not be the most promising type of tag to use either.

NOTE: **Know Your Break-Even Point**

Show only the service area that you really want to serve—where it's easy and affordable for you to serve new customers. You can still serve existing customers, and high-value new customers, outside your service area.

The current price of tags—$25 a month—might not sound like a lot of money. However, for tags to pay for themselves, they have to bring in $25 of extra profit—not extra revenue—per month. Let's say you're running a specialty grocery store with a $10 average spend per customer visit and a 5% profit margin. That means you make 50 cents per customer visit, and that your tags need to generate 50 customer visits per month just to break even. (Be sure to count repeat as well as first-time visits resulting from the tag.) Figure out the break-even point for tags in your business before you invest, and track progress toward it on your Dashboard, as described in the next chapter.

Signing Up for Tags

Turning on tags requires that you already have a verified Google Places listing, as described in Lesson 5, "Claiming Your Google Places Page." You must also have a credit or debit card handy to pay for the monthly fee that goes into effect after the initial one-month trial offer is up, should you decide to continue.

CAUTION: **Tags Not Available in All Areas**

Tags might not yet be available in your area. At this writing, Google doesn't provide forward-looking information about the availability of tags in different localities. So if you don't have tags available to you yet, you may not know when they will become available until they do.

After you have a verified listing and a credit or debit card handy, follow these steps to create a tag:

1. Go to http://www.google.com and sign in to the Google account associated with your business. Choose **Settings**, **Google Account Settings**. From the list of Google products that appears, choose **Google Places**. Your Google Places Dashboard opens.

2. For the listing you want to update, click **Create Tag**. Your listing's Dashboard page opens.

3. Scroll down to the listing tags area, which has the same yellow marker as tags do. Find the Preview and Select a Tag drop-down menu, as shown in Figure 11.3.

   You may have an offer for a free 30-day trial of Google Tags, in which case your first 30 days of use will be free.

4. Choose the type of tag you want to preview.

   A preview of the tag appears, as shown in Google Maps results and text search results (see Figure 11.3).

5. Keep trying different tag types to see what they look like.

   If you want to add a feature to your Google Places listing so that you can tag it, exit signing up for tags and add the feature, as described in previous lessons.

6. When you're ready to create your tag, click the **Proceed to Billing** button. The billing screen opens.

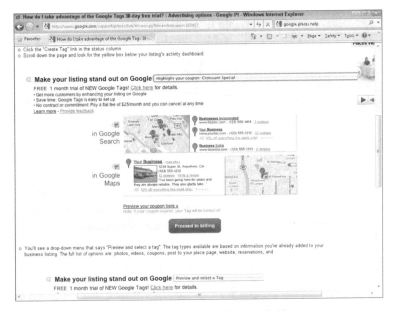

FIGURE 11.3   You can preview every type of tag available to you.

7. Enter your billing information and read the program terms. When
    have finished, click the button, **I accept. Activate My Tag for
    $25 Per Month**.

    Your tag should show up alongside your listing on Google within
    a few hours.

8. To change your tag, repeat steps 1–5, and then activate the tag.

Using AdWords to Increase Business

AdWords is a huge moneymaker for Google—and for the businesses that
use it (otherwise they wouldn't bother). An AdWords ad is the modern
equivalent of a TV ad back in the *Mad Men* era of the early 1960s, when

ad agencies on Madison Avenue in New York were thought to have the key to unlock the desires of consumers. Today, the same kind of money is being made with AdWords ads. Figure 11.4 shows several AdWords ads. An AdWords ad is search relevant, just like search listings. So, you can buy into a search term such as *terrapins*, and make it globally, nationally, or locally relevant. When someone searches for *terrapins* on Google, your ad is likely to show up. Of course, if a lot of people want that search term, you'll have to pay more to get your AdWords ad up at the top—or even to appear at all.

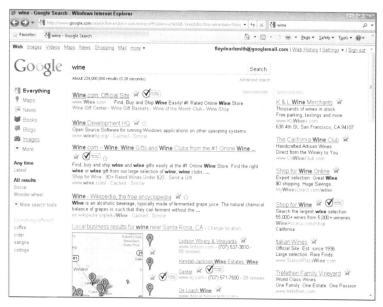

FIGURE 11.4 AdWords gives you a shot at grabbing a share of search traffic.

> NOTE: **Get a Quick Introduction to Adwords**
>
> For a fast, efficient introduction to Google AdWords by this author, see *Sams Teach Yourself Google AdWords in 10 Minutes* by Bud Smith (Sams, 2010).

The good news about AdWords is that it follows an approach called *pay per click*. You have to pay for your ad only when someone clicks it! Think of all the great, free branding you get from people seeing your ad but not clicking it at that time. They could easily find you later through the usual kind of search (called *organic* search), and Google wouldn't get a penny. The bad news, though, is that Google tracks this. If no one ever clicks your ad, Google gradually drops it down in search listings, compared to other ads that get more clicks. So, you lose that free branding as your ad gets less and less useful. You have to improve the ad text so that it gets more clicks or increase the amount you pay per click to have Google raise the profile of your ad, maximizing your clickthroughs and Google's revenue. If you want to be the kingpin of terrapins, either with a web-based business or a chain of terrapin shops, or a combination, AdWords just might be the key to helping you do it. Many businesses are making big bucks through the inspired use of AdWords. As competition heats up, though, some are struggling to make their AdWords buys worthwhile. Creating AdWords ads, tracking their success over time, and improving the ads and offers is a big project. Figure 11.5 shows a representative screen from the AdWords control panel.

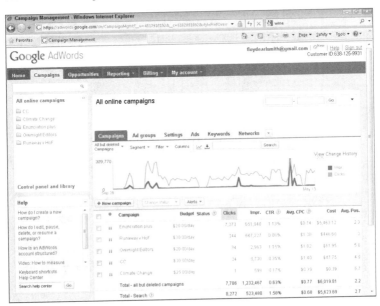

FIGURE 11.5   You might find yourself working hard to get your AdWords right.

In many ways, creating your Google Places page, various features, and tags is good preparation for AdWords. Together, Google Places, a website for your organization, and AdWords create a powerful combination. Use this book to get your Google Places page right, and then consider diving fully into AdWords to see whether you can really cash in.

> TIP: **Customized Landing Pages**
>
> Google AdWords ads always link to a web page. You can use your Google Places page as the destination of an AdWords ad, but it's much more common—and probably more effective—to link to a customized landing page on your website instead. Linking to your Google Places page is a quick-and-dirty solution if you want to get involved with AdWords in a hurry.

Summary

In this lesson, you learned how to use tags in Google Places and received a brief introduction to Google AdWords. You saw how advertising can increase your business and what tags are available for your Google Places page in Google text search and Google Maps search. You then saw how Google AdWords can help you get more online traffic for your business.

LESSON 12
Using the Dashboard

In this lesson, you learn what the graphs and statistics shown in your Google Places Dashboard mean. You see how to change the date range for which graphs and statistics are shown, plus how to track data over time, as well as how to make changes to get better results—in your statistics and in your business.

Tracking Your Google Places Dashboard Results

In the preceding lesson, I mentioned that businesspeople usually know that half their advertising spending is wasted—but that they never know which half. With Google Places, though, most of the advertising value you get is free, for the Google Places listing itself, or inexpensive, in the case of tags (as described in the preceding lesson). Not only that, but Google Places actually gives you a way to know how effective your advertising is, in the form of the Google Places Dashboard.

NOTE: **Check Out Data Mining**

Businesses are getting more and more value and differentiation from using data about their current and potential customers in new and interesting ways. This data mining is usually unavailable to small and local businesses, but the Google Places Dashboard gives you a way in. You might derive a lot of value from the time and effort you spend on it.

What You See

When you sign in to your Dashboard, as described in the next section, you see a graph with your listing's activity; Figure 12.1 shows an example. The graph shows two lines:

▶ **Impressions:** This is the number of times that a Google.com or Google Maps search caused your business listing to appear in a search results screen.

▶ **Actions:** This is the number of times people interacted with the listing—the number of times they looked at a coupon, clicked through to your website, or got driving directions.

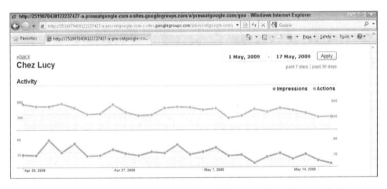

FIGURE 12.1   Your Dashboard shows what's happening with your listing.

You can see exact numbers for Impressions and Actions below the graph. You can also enter an exact date range to make the graph and statistics specific, or click Last 7 Days or Last 30 Days to see the graph and statistics for the relevant dates. The Dashboard also shows two additional pieces of information:

▶ **Top Search Queries:** This is a list of the specific search terms that users entered that led them to see your listing. It tells you just how users got to results with your listing in them.

▶ **ZIP Codes Where Driving Directions Come From:** This shows the ZIP codes that users who got driving directions come from.

On the right side of the Dashboard, you see links to follow to edit your business listing, to get tips on improving your listing, and to upload additional listings if you have them.

> TIP: **Increasing Directions Requests**
>
> You might see a spike in driving direction requests from faraway places if you post a Help Wanted ad, or a special that really beats the heck out of the competition!

What You Get

The numbers on your Dashboard are a bit of a hall of mirrors; nothing in them means just what it seems to mean! Here's a bit of analysis to help you understand what you're really getting from your Dashboard stats. You have to look at different stats together to understand what they mean to your business:

- ▶ **Impressions versus top search queries:** The impressions you see can be quite relevant or quite irrelevant; it's the search queries used that make a difference. If you run a wine shop, searches for *wine*, for example, are quite relevant to you. But if you run a wine distributorship, they're not. Compare your impressions to your top search queries, taking the nature of your business into account, to understand how relevant your impressions are likely to be.

- ▶ **Impressions versus actions:** You want people who see your listing to act on it, but this is likely to happen only when they really are searching for a business like yours. Among people who are doing such a search, you can improve the percentage who act on your listing; see the next section for some ideas. You can also track specific action versus impressions.

- ▶ **ZIP codes versus customer locations:** The list of ZIP codes where driving directions come from can be misleading. It shows the origins of people *who get driving directions*. Nearby customers are unlikely to bother, except if they happen to be coming to you from work or a trip out of town, which will be misleading.

The ZIP codes shown mostly represent where your relatively far-away customers are coming from, not where your average customer is coming from. And they represent only a fraction of the faraway customers because many of them won't need to get driving directions. The farthest-away customers are the most likely to need directions, and so will be overrepresented in your results. The ZIP code listing does have a use. If you see one or more clusters of visitors, you can consider starting a new location there, supporting customers with delivery services, or other ways to increase your sales in that area.

> TIP: **Don't Act Too Quickly!**
> The ZIP codes listing in your Dashboard is only an indicator of where you might find new customers. You'd want to survey customers, check out the competition (and why your customers might be bypassing other businesses that are closer by), and perhaps take other steps before making important decisions that affect your bottom line.

Using Your Dashboard

Using the Dashboard properly is a key to getting the most out of Google Places. It's also good preparation for using more advanced tracking services, in particular the tracking capabilities of Google AdWords, described in Lesson 11, "Advertising with Tags and AdWords."

Seeing and Changing the Dashboard Display

Google Places gives you a small thumbnail of your statistics in the Dashboard, but you can click through to get much more detail for impressions, actions, and, if you use them, Google Tags results. Follow these steps:

1. Go to http://www.google.com and sign in to the Google account associated with your business. Choose **Settings**, **Google Account Settings**. From the list of Google products that appears, choose

Google Places. Your Google Places Dashboard opens, including a thumbnail of your visit statistics.

2. For the listing you want to update, click the listing name. Your listing's Dashboard page opens, as shown in Figure 12.1 earlier in this lesson.

3. Examine the activity and impressions. To see results for the last 7 days, or the last 30 days, click the respective link. The display will update with charts covering the specified period. In addition to the graph, the numbers and other information below will update as well, including impressions, actions, search queries, and so on.

TIP: **Get Daily Results**

To get impressions or actions for a given day, roll the mouse over the spot on the appropriate graph representing that day.

---

4. To see results for a specific period, click one of the dates at the top of the page, above last 7 days | last 30 days. Using the calendar that appears, select a start date and an end date, and then click **Apply**.

As with the links for last 7 days and last 30 days, the display will update with charts and numbers covering the specified period.

TIP: **Spotting Trends**

Enter periods of time that are multiples of weeks to spot trends by day of the week, which might relate to workdays/schooldays. Enter periods of time that encompass several entire months to spot trends by day of the month, which might relate to paydays, for example.

---

5. Examine the totals, top search queries, and driving directions requests for the period you've specified.

To get data for a single date at a time, make the start and end dates the same. Consider copying the information into a spreadsheet for further analysis—a painstaking, but potentially rewarding, process.

6. If you use Google Tags, scroll down to the Tags area, as shown in Figure 12.2.

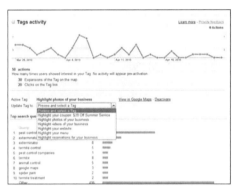

FIGURE 12.2   Google tags have their own report in the Dashboard.

Impressions and actions for your sponsored tags appear. You can use this data to assign a cost per action for the actions taken in response to your tags. If you change the tag content and get report data to match, you can compare tags against each other.

> NOTE: **Look at Actions/Impressions Ratios**
> Although it's great to get impressions and actions results, it's also valuable to have actions as a percentage of impressions. After all, getting 10 actions from 10 impressions is pretty good, whereas getting 10 actions from 1,000 impressions is not very noteworthy! Consider using the results from Google Places in a spreadsheet or other program that will enable you to calculate actions per impression and other important ratios.

Improving Your Results

Your Google Places listing is a big opportunity to get customers, so anything you can do to improve your results is a good thing. However,

Google Places addresses only some parts of the chain from noncustomer to customer. Let's look at each step along the way and how Google Places can help:

▶ **Awareness:** It's literally impossible for people to become your customers if they aren't aware of you—and the stronger that awareness is, the more chance you have of making a sale. This is where Google Places is so great: It gets you awareness, by inclusion in search listings, among people who might never or rarely think of you. Use the top search queries to find terms that you can include in your Google Places listing, website, and other online marketing to improve your search results. See Lesson 14, "Improving Search Engine Results," for details.

▶ **Actions:** You want people who see your listing to buy from you, and their actions with the listing are an indicator of whether that happens. Not an exclusive indicator, however—the user could just make a mental note to come see you, and do it, without interacting with your listing. To get more interactions, though, you can get a higher search results listing, more reviews, and a better quote (see Lesson 14), or add a tag (see Lesson 11).

▶ **Calling or visiting (first time):** Turning someone who interacts with your business listing into someone who interacts with you by phone or in person is valuable. Everything about your listing can improve or detract from your odds of getting customers. Use this entire book to improve your listing, and thereby your odds of getting a new customer from your online presence.

▶ **Calling or visiting (repeat visits):** Hopefully, you treat people so well that they no longer use Google Search or Google Maps to find a business like yours—they just keep coming to you! However, if they do search, the earlier steps involving actions, as well as how well you serve and treat your customers, will all make a difference.

These are not the only stats that matter, of course. There are many different levers you can grasp to improve your online presence and your business results. There are also various services out there for measuring all these aspects. One such service is Localvisibility.org; this site automatically analyzes your use of keywords, your listing on social media services such as Facebook and Twitter, and your competitive positioning. An example of a Localvisibility listing is shown in Figure 12.3. Try this service for your own business, but consider focusing on your Google Places listing first, before looking into the broader range of services and characteristics included in a Localvisibility listing.

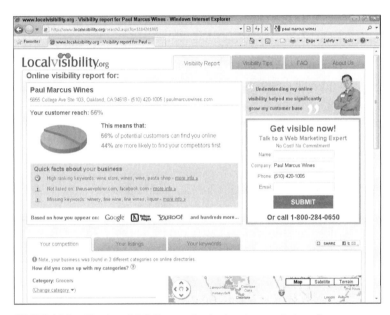

FIGURE 12.3　The Localvisibility service looks at your whole online presence.

Tracking Your Results

You can get a lot of value out of your Google Places listing by tracking a few key statistics. Each has its own special considerations, and its own value.

Real-World Events

You'll often see a change in a key statistic, such as impressions, and be aware of a reason for it. You might get a spike in impressions just after a news story mentioning your shop or the overall business you're in. Note the date and nature of important real-world events so that you can look for correlations between events and your stats.

Changes You Make

Along with real-world events, changes you make in your online presence, in offline advertising, and in your actual business can all make a difference in your results. Write down each change you make in a list that you can keep referring to. Note the date, the change (in detail), and any thoughts about the reason for the change, as well as whether you thought that it made a difference.

Impressions

People spend a lot of time working on their search engine positioning (see Lesson 14), and impressions are a measure of the results. You can track your impressions over time or recover them from the statistics in Google Places. You should track your website visits separately to tie them together.

Actions

As with impressions, you can track actions over time or recover them from the statistics in Google Places. You should track actions from your website separately to tie them all together.

Business Results

You'll naturally track your business results—sales, profits, and so on—in some detail for accounting and tax purposes. You might want to fine-tune your tracking, though, so that you can do more detailed analysis. Daily tracking is needed to tie changes in your online presence to your business results; if you make frequent changes, or have other reasons for detailed analysis, even tracking by time of day can be useful. (Discovering that you frequently have a surge of business in a specific "day part," for instance, can influence your marketing and staffing.) Figure out just how closely you want to track your business results soon after you start using Google Places so that you have the information you need to compare actions to outcomes.

Bringing It All Together

You might benefit from establishing a regular routine of bringing information together to learn what you can from it and make changes in your business and marketing to improve results. You might want to set goals for one or more metrics to manage your business against. The most important metric for most businesses is profitability; it's rarely worth continuing if you're not making money. Nonprofits and government agencies are likely to have important financial measures too, such as performance against budget. After you're tracking profitability, budget performance, or some other key metric, try to figure out what contributes most strongly to it for your operation. Also think about low-hanging fruit. For instance, getting more customers is good, but so is improving your revenue from existing customers. Where do you have the most promising opportunities?

Summary

In this lesson, you learned what the graphs and statistics shown in your Google Places Dashboard mean. You learned how to change the date range for which graphs and statistics are shown, how to track data over time, and how to make changes to get better results—in your statistics and in your business.

LESSON 13

Using QR Codes and Getting Better Reviews

In this lesson, you learn how to generate, use, and publicize QR codes for your business. In addition, you learn how to make reviews on your Google Places site work for you, how to leave reviews of your own, and how to respond to others' reviews on your website.

Understanding QR Codes

A Quick Response code, or QR code, is a graphical code for representing a lot of text in a small, square space. It's basically a denser, square barcode, like the kind you see on all sorts of products, and that checkout clerks use to scan products that you buy at the supermarket and elsewhere. Google Pages uses QR codes to represent URLs. Using a QR code and an app on a mobile phone, users can take a picture and be taken straight to a web page, without having to enter a URL. A detailed description and examples of QR codes are available on Wikipedia at http://en.wikipedia.org/wiki/QR_Code, as shown in Figure 13.1.

Mobile phone apps that read QR codes often also read barcodes. These apps can either seamlessly open a web page when they encounter a QR code, or give you information about a product when they encounter a barcode. Figure 13.2 shows the Barcode Scanner app on Android recognizing a QR code displayed in the Wikipedia article mentioned earlier.

Although QR codes are used elsewhere, Google has made QR codes a kind of symbol for Google Places, offering premade QR codes in the Google Places Dashboard. Google has even proactively sent posters with QR codes to businesses that qualify for the Favorite Places program, as described in Lesson 14, "Improving Search Engine Results."

FIGURE 13.1   QR codes are popular with computer nerds and Google.

FIGURE 13.2   An Android app quickly recognizes a QR code.

You can jump on the Google Places bandwagon for QR codes by printing out a poster with your Google Places QR code and putting it in your window and other customer-accessible places. Many of your customers will be able to scan it with an app on their mobile phones. It will bring up your Google Places page with information about your business.

For a customer to use a QR code to bring up a page of information might seem kind of redundant during business hours, when the user could just ask you or one of your employees. However, people like gadgets so much these days that they'll do it. More to the point, they can use the QR code when you're closed for business. If the information they find is to their liking, it might increase the odds that they'll come back.

You can also incorporate the QR code as a graphic on your web page. You can display it without comment, for the cognoscenti to use, or you can offer an explanation of QR codes or Google Places, helping educate your web visitors and customers. Either way, you're bringing more attention to your Google Places page, and possibly increasing your search engine ranking as well.

Your QR code can also go on marketing brochures and other pieces that you put out. It serves two purposes. It helps customers geek out in a way that supports their getting information about your business, and identifies you and your business as being tech savvy, making sensible use of both QR codes and Google Places.

Using QR Codes

You can easily get an image of your QR code from your Google Places Dashboard. Just follow these steps:

1. Go to http://www.google.com and sign in to the Google account associated with your business. Choose **Settings**, **Google Account Settings**. From the list of Google products that appears, choose **Google Places**. If you have multiple listings, click the one you want. The Google Places Dashboard for your listing opens.

TIP: **Make Your Own QR Code**

You can generate your own QR code for the URL of your Google Places page as well as using the one provided to you on your Google Places Dashboard. Just search online for a term such as *QR code generator* to find a suitable program online.

2. Scroll down to see your QR code. Your QR code shows on the Dashboard. Figure 13.3 shows an example.

FIGURE 13.3   Your QR code is embedded on your Dashboard.

3. Click the **About QR Codes** link to learn more about QR codes from Google.

4. To use your QR code elsewhere, you can copy and paste the image from your Dashboard to another program on your website and other online locations where it won't be reproduced, and needs to be small—and where users can bring their mobile phone close. The image on your Dashboard is just about the smallest image that will work reliably, and you should test it yourself before using it too widely.

You may need a small version of your QR code for your website, stationery, and so on. For this kind of purpose, the version of your QR code that appears in your Dashboard is just big enough to be useful. So, if you need a small version of the QR code, just copy and paste the image from your Dashboard. Don't shrink it any further, or it might not be recognizable to some apps, which would frustrate the people trying to use it.

5. To use your QR code on a poster or for other business uses, even where it needs to be small, click the **Print QR Poster** link. Print the poster or copy the QR code for other uses.

A poster with the QR code appears, as shown in Figure 13.4. To use the QR code in a small size, consider keeping it at least

10×10 in size, and surrounding it by a border of whitespace. This makes it easier for mobile phone cameras to autofocus on it.

FIGURE 13.4 You can print your own poster, complete with your QR code.

CAUTION: **Don't Save QR Codes as JPEGs**

Avoid saving images of QR codes in JPEG format. JPEG is great for shrinking files, but it generates visual noise that interferes with the recognizability of QR codes. Use a lossless file format such as GIF or PNG.

Making Reviews Work for You

Easily the most frustrating thing about Google Places, and other services such as CitySearch, Trip Advisor, Yahoo! Local, and Yelp (shown in Figure 13.5), is user reviews. (All these businesses are used as sources for reviews on Google Places, as well.) With no filter, no editing, and complete anonymity, users can log on and leave a positive—or devastatingly negative—review.

FIGURE 13.5   Many business owners "yelp" about their online reviews.

Reviews are ranked by algorithms—that is, by rules embedded in software programs, based on the machine's recognizing, or not recognizing, certain words. There's no human intervention, so complaining to the humans at Google, if you can even get one to communicate with you about it, is unlikely to do much good.

As one blogger put it, "Small businesses are engaged (and often enraged) with reviews on their Google Places Pages…. The forums are rife with over-the-top pleas, cajolings, and complaints about reviews on their Places Page" (see http://www.blumenthals.com for this and other comments about Google Places). The negative reviews drive business owners nuts. It's easy to imagine a potential customer bypassing you entirely because of just one negative review. Having a few of them—let alone having them dominate your overall list of reviews—can really, really hurt. And there's almost nothing you can do. Oh, you can improve your customer service, fix specific complaints, even clean up the shop, and lower your prices. Nothing will get rid of negative reviews. You can only hope to get many new, better ones, gradually burying the bad news under a slew of good news.

Well, there is one thing you can do to help yourself: Respond to reviews, as described next. That's right—Google lets you reply to reviews (but only to replies left by Google users directly on Google Places, not to reviews scraped from the Trip Advisors and Yelps of the world). I'll give details on how to reply, and what to say, next.

Almost as bad as bad reviews is no review. Users seem to take the number of reviews as a sign of a business's overall popularity and effectiveness. There's an old quote from theatrical legend George M. Cohan: "I don't care what you say about me, as long as you say something about me, and as long as you spell my name right." Everyone on Google Places will spell your name right, and you want them to say something, as long as it's not too negative. Here are some tips for getting good reviews—and handling bad ones:

▶ **Start strong:** It's easy for me to say this, but the best defense is a good offense. If you already have good customer service and are responsive to problems that do arise, you're unlikely to get negative reviews.

▶ **See what they're saying about you already:** Do a Google search for your business name. Look up your business on CitySearch, Trip Advisor, Yahoo! Local, and Yelp, as well as alternative and local services. Bring all the feedback together.

▶ **Get candid opinions from friends, family, and customers:** Ask friends, family, and customers with whom you have a good relationship to tell you the worst things about your business—and then the best things. Take notes. Prioritize the feedback so that you can reduce the negative and accentuate the positive.

▶ **Ask for complaints:** Find ways to encourage complaints from customers to go directly to you, instead of directly online, such as putting a feedback form in a prominent place. Then follow up! Try to find ways to connect back to the original complainant to let them know they've been heard and, if appropriate, that their complaint has been acted on.

▶ **Take action:** Try to understand each and every concern and complaint, as well as each and every positive comment. What might have caused each one? Is there anything you can do now to prevent similar complaints from recurring—and to encourage more positive responses? (This can require drastic steps—maybe letting an employee go, changing a supplier or two, and cleaning, cleaning, cleaning.)

▶ **Encourage online feedback:** Now that you've (more or less literally) cleaned up your act, encourage customer feedback. You can link to feedback opportunities from your Google Places page and your website, post a sign in your shop, and ask customers (especially happy ones) to post feedback wherever you think it will do the most good

Leaving Reviews

If you're going to be getting reviews, you might as well know what users have to do to leave one. Follow these steps to post a review on Google Places:

1. Use Google Search or Google Maps to search for a local business or other organization that you've enjoyed dealing with in the past.

   Start with a positive review, and think hard—and sympathetically, as a Google Places page holder—before posting negative ones.

2. Click the **More Info** link next to the business name. The Google Places page appears.

3. Click the link and write a review.

4. Add a title and rating to the review. Be positive and brief in the title; be kind in the rating.

5. Click **Save**.

6. To change the nickname that appears, click your personal information in Google Accounts, and you can change and save your nickname there.

You shouldn't need to do this in most cases, but if you really must warn the public of dire customer service or other problems, you might want to use a different nickname for that posting.

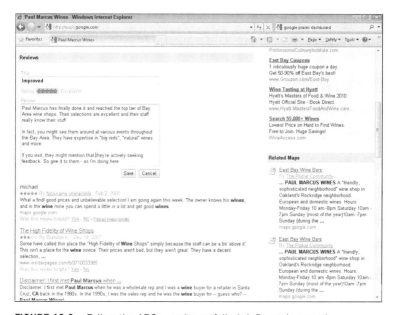

FIGURE 13.6 Follow the ABCs—write artfully, briefly, and correctly.

Responding to Reviews on Your Places Page

In response to what seems to have been intense demand from holders of Google Places pages, verified owners are now allowed to respond to reviews. You can't respond to reviews scraped from sites such as CitySearch; you have to go to that site and use its response or complaint mechanisms, if any. Whatever you accomplish on the other site might not cause any change in the content on your Google Places page.

When you do respond to complaints on your Google Places page, though, you literally demonstrate responsiveness. Here are some suggestions on what to do with the ability to respond:

▶ **Think of it as an opportunity:** Every complainant probably represents others who never spoke up. This is the chance to demonstrate to all of them how well you handle feedback—and to fix the underlying problem, once and for all.

▶ **Be nice, and be polite:** You're speaking for your business or organization, not as an individual. Keep it upbeat.

▶ **Be professional:** Check your spelling and grammar—and then double-check it. Despite the prevalence of txtspk and other linguistic abominations, proper English is still the preferred mode for businesses to use with customers.

▶ **Be brief:** Write a draft response, print it out, and then take a red pencil to it. Just give the basics. Three sentences should be enough for most responses.

▶ **Don't be "salesy":** Pass up the opportunity to mention this month's special. Write as a trusted expert on your business's area of focus, not as a salesperson.

▶ **Thank people:** Feedback, even harsh feedback, is a gift. Be appreciative of it. (But don't thank fairly generic positive commenters individually, lest you crowd out more specific, and more useful, feedback.)

Follow these steps to respond to a review:

1. Go to http://www.google.com and sign in to the Google account associated with your business. Choose **Settings**, **Google Account Settings**. From the list of Google products that appears, choose **Google Places**. If you have multiple listings, click the one you want.

2. On the right, where it reads Respond to Reviews, click **Reviews**. The Google Places Dashboard for your listing opens.

3. Scroll down to the reviews section. You'll see reviews left on Google Maps only, not reviews from other sources. Select a review to respond to, and then click the link, **Respond Publicly As the Owner**.

   An area appears for you to enter your response.

4. Enter your response. Consider spell-checking and grammar-checking your response in a word processing program, sharing it with others, and even having a professional proofreader look at it before proceeding.

5. Click **Publish**. The response will appear publicly, as a response from the owner, on your Google Places page.

CAUTION: **Get Permission!**

If you are not the owner, be sure to get the owner's approval before posting a contribution—it will appear as a response from the owner, so you need the owner's agreement if at all possible, for the complainant's sake as well as your own.

Summary

In this lesson, you learned how to generate, use, and publicize QR codes for your business. In addition, you learned how to make reviews on your Google Places site work for you, how to leave reviews of your own, and how to respond to others' reviews on your website.

LESSON 14

Improving Search Engine Results

*In this lesson, you learn how to help your business become a Google
Favorite Place, how to understand and improve search engine results
relating to your business, and how to create a basic website with the help
of a provider.*

Becoming a Google Favorite Place

A Google Favorite Place is simply a business that Google chooses to favor
with a window decal, as shown in Figure 14.1, that says the business is,
well, a Google Favorite Place. The decal also displays the business's QR
code, as described in Lesson 13, "Using QR Codes and Getting Better
Reviews."

CAUTION: **Take Care of Your Sticker!**
Be careful with your Favorite Place sticker if you get one. It's very
tough to get a replacement from Google because each one is cus-
tom-made to feature the QR code for the specific business that
receives it, and Google doesn't want extra copies floating around
where they might not belong.

Your business is chosen as a Favorite Place based on the popularity of
your Google Places listing, according to Google. You'll find Favorite
Places in big cities, small towns, and rural areas. However, there's no clear
guideline as to just how popular you need to be to be chosen—whether it
depends on your location, type of business, and so on, or how often
Google will evaluate Google Places listings against the standards. (Google

has revealed that about 100,000 U.S. businesses have received Favorite Places recognition so far, out of the estimated 28 million U.S. businesses total.)

FIGURE 14.1   Becoming a Favorite Place is an honor.

TIP: **Google Changes the Rules Often**

Google frequently changes the algorithms (the rules in its software) that determine search engine results, so don't be surprised if your business's search engine results change for seemingly no reason. However, Google is always trying to pursue accurate measures of popularity for each site on the Web. So, a concerted effort over time should raise your search engine results even as the underlying algorithms shift.

There's a bit of a rich-get-richer effect, too, because businesses that have early success on the Web—including, perhaps, receiving a Favorite Places poster when they were first made available a couple of years ago—have a lot of incentive to keep investing in their Google Places page and their overall web presence. These early winners also get more online traffic due to that self-same Favorite Places decal. So, if you're coming into the game late, your chances are not that good.

Don't despair, though. Using the information in this book, you can improve your Google Places listing, and set yourself a goal of receiving Favorite Places recognition. Whether you win or not, the work you do will help build up your online presence, and hopefully bring you more business—the ultimate reward for a local business owner.

TIP: **Make Use of Your Google Maps Poster**

The We're on Google Maps poster, described in Lesson 13, which any business can print out, shows your QR code. It's a pretty good substitute for the Favorite Place poster, until such time as Google chooses to favor you with one of those, too.

Understanding Search Engine Results

A high ranking in Google Search results is a huge help for a business or other organization. It brings in new business—and helps improve the search ranking further, in a kind of self-fulfilling prophecy.

Search engine rankings are based on a constantly changing secret formula that Google keeps a closely guarded secret. That's because Google wants the search engine rankings to reflect how popular a website really is with web users. But business owners and experts in search engine optimization (SEO) want a quick hit to get their business high in the rankings, even if it's not really popular. So, business owners and SEO consultants use the details of Google's methods, if they can, to "game" the system and move their business up the charts.

Figure 14.2 shows the results of a recent search for *search engine optimization* on Google. You can see that there are plenty of Google AdWords ads, courses, books, and more. Try the search yourself; you'll be amazed by the depth and variety of the results.

FIGURE 14.2 *Search engine optimization* is a popular search term.

The basics of Google's methods, though, have been widely discussed. The "secret sauce" is to give a website credit if a lot of people visit it—and if other popular websites link to it. For a business with a poor search engine ranking, this is pernicious. A website for a business that has been around for a while, and perhaps got on the Web early, will have lots of links—in business directories, articles, blog postings, and so forth. This helps the search engine ranking, which helps the business get found online, which leads to more traffic, more links, and so on.

The Favorite Places designation is part of the problem, as well. A business with a fairly popular website can easily boost its Google Places designation just by linking to its Google Places page from its website (and vice versa). All those preexisting connections now help boost the Google Places page as well as the business's main website. Once again, the rich get richer, and the poor get poorer.

CAUTION: **Think Before You Pay**

Don't spend money on SEO unless you're very clear on what you're going to get out of it. Getting a higher search engine ranking is gratifying, but try the easy, free methods described here, and in other books and articles, first. It's only worth investing larger amounts of time and money if you're very clear just how a higher search engine ranking will bring in more revenue, profit, or other desirable results.

Improving Search Engine Results

You can do myriad things to improve your Google search placement, and you can easily spend a great deal of time and money doing so—probably to the detriment of your actual business. Some simple things, however, are quite basic, and are highly likely to contribute to both your search engine ranking and your actual business success. Consider these tips:

▶ **Get your Google Places listing right:** A strong Google Places listing is easier to achieve than a strong web presence and helps all around. Use the information throughout this book to create and improve your Google Places listing. Use the list in your Dashboard to find any areas where your listing is incomplete, and add them in to get a 100% completeness listing.

▶ **Create/improve your website:** Find websites you like for businesses similar to yours, and use those as models for what you want in a site. Learn how to create a site yourself, or get recommendations for a good provider to create and host the site for you. (One such provider is shown in Figure 14.3.) Don't try to do too much too fast; just improve your website steadily over time.

▶ **Tie your Google Places listing and your website together:** Point to your website from your Google Places listing, and create links the other way as well. Create picture libraries on sites such as Flickr, and create pointers among your Google Places listing, your website, and Flickr.

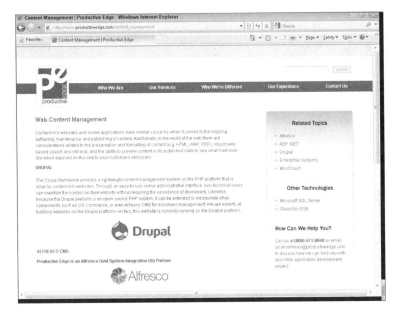

FIGURE 14.3   Providers stand ready to help improve your website.

▶ **Improve your online reviews:** Improve your online reviews, as described in Lesson 13. This encourages people to visit your (new and improved) website and Google Places page.

▶ **Get links from others:** Don't ask for links to a crummy website; improve your site, and then ask for (and offer) links. This is the single biggest step toward improving your search engine rankings, but it's a later step, not an early one.

▶ **Be consistent and repetitive:** Get your company name, address, phone info, keywords, and basic "what we do" blurb into a consistent form, and then put them in as many (sensible) places as possible—directories, blogs, Facebook, and so on.

▶ **Don't be evil:** An SEO consultant might try to convince you to use black hat techniques—basically, tricks—to try to cheat on your search engine ranking. If you do, and you're caught, Google will pull your content from its search results for a long time to come.

▶ **Use tags and Google AdWords:** Don't spend money to bring people to a crummy Google Places page or website. After you improve them, though, both Google Places tags and Google AdWords are a quick-and-dirty way to increase your traffic, as described in Lesson 11, "Advertising with Tags and AdWords." Over time, figure out just how tags and AdWords are adding to your bottom line and adjust your spending to match.

CAUTION: **AdWords Ads and Organic Search Results**

When you improve your search engine ranking by improving your site, and also buy Google AdWords, you'll find that sometimes your AdWords ad and your organic search engine result appear on the same page. And yes, users will sometimes click the AdWords ad (which costs you money) instead of the organic search engine result (which is free to click). You just have to accept it as a cost of doing business and be happy for the attention, even if some of it costs you money.

Creating a Basic Website with a Provider

You can easily create a basic website yourself using one of the many website-building applications available online. However, most of us lack the technical and graphical skill to actually create a website that looks professional and works well.

Therefore, you might want to hire a service provider to create a website with you. Notice I didn't say *for* you but *with* you. You want to partner with your providers, not let them run riot online by themselves, with your business's reputation, as well as your checking account balance, at stake. Follow these steps to create a solid basic website with a provider:

1. Do a really good job on your Google Places page, as described in this book. The things you learn, the information you gather, and the results will all help you do a better job with your website.

2. Check your search engine results, and take notes. Do some testing of your search engine results on key search terms, and see how competitors—both local and national—do on the same terms. Save the results for later comparisons.

3. Gather your current marketing materials and printouts of your current website, if any, and those of competitors as well. Identify images, approaches, and descriptions you like.

4. Create a simple chart showing the web pages that you want to have, showing the title, listing any key content, and showing connections.

   You can have your provider help with this, but it's better if you try it first yourself—so that you have a better idea of what you want and why, before you get too much outside influence.

   For an example, see Figure 14.4. The example includes a line where the "fold" in a web page is—the part that's visible on a typical screen without having to scroll down. The next step in the design process would be to rough out what kind of content would appear on each page.

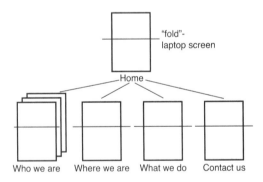

FIGURE 14.4   A simple diagram done early can greatly improve your future website.

5. Ask friendly businesspeople about their own experience in creating websites and providers they like, as well as what they paid. When listening to your friends' experience, look for a confluence of a good working experience, a reasonable price, and a good website as a result.

6. Interview several providers. Identify a few likely providers and interview them. Look for someone who does their homework

before you meet, who listens more than they speak, and who seems to want to get the job done in a reasonable amount of time. Also, look at past results and be sure that they meet your criteria for a good website. Give extra marks for someone who shows a good understanding of SEO. Your favored provider should also know something about Google Places and how it can work with your website.

7. Ask for and approve an overall design, wireframes, and each page as it's completed. Don't just let your provider run off and create something you don't like and then charge you to redo the whole thing. "Go slow to go fast"—get lots of opportunities for feedback and review early on so that the finish can be quick and the resulting website something you're proud of.

8. Get feedback on the site before and after launch. Don't expect to create the world's greatest website on your first or second try. Just make sure the site reflects well on your business and has as few obvious mistakes as possible. Check it carefully before launch and again after launch—you might be amazed at what you find the second time through.

9. Keep checking your search engine results—and keep notes. Keep testing your search engine results, and see whether they improve. Take the steps described in the previous section to improve them as well. Track the results; you'll get good ideas for further improvements to your website, and perhaps even to your underlying business.

> **NOTE: There's No Substitute for a Good Website**
> Having an improved website inspires visitors to spend more time and click more links within your site, and others to link to it, all of which should gradually improve your search engine results.

Summary

In this lesson, you learned how to help your business become a Google Favorite Place, how to understand and improve search engine results relating to your business, and how to create a basic website with the help of a provider.

APPENDIX A

Places Categories

One of the most important decisions you'll make about your Google Places page is the category or categories in which it will be listed. Categories are important because they are used for several purposes:

▶ Supporting search in Google Search, Google Maps, and elsewhere

▶ Supporting Nearby Places You Might Like and Related Maps on your Google Places page

▶ Direct display of the category or categories on your Google Places page

To specify categories—you can use up to five, and one of them must be a category from Google's list—you enter them while editing your Google Places page, as described in Lesson 2, "Editing Your Google Places Page." However, knowing just what category or categories to enter can be tricky. And, if you get it wrong, the ability of web users to find you online could be compromised.

Your search engine ranking—that is, how high up in the search results list your business appears, considering the relevance of the search and how local to you the search is—is very important. For search on a personal computer, being in the top few results when you should be is very important; for search on a mobile phone, with a much smaller screen, slower online connections, and impatient users, it's crucial.

There's an entire practice called *search engine optimization* (SEO) that focuses exclusively on search engine results. Getting your organization's categories right is an important step in getting a strong search engine ranking.

> TIP: **Learn All About SEO**
>
> To learn more about SEO as well as a many other web marketing activities, pick up a copy of *The Ultimate Web Marketing Guide* by Michael Miller (published by Que). It has everything you need to know to get started.

Finding Categories That Google Places Supports

Google Places supports a wide range of categories, but there's no definitive list that you can look at. Instead, you enter part of a category name, and Google shows a drop-down list of matching categories, as described in Lesson 2. If you don't know to enter a specific term, you might not ever find a category that you should, indeed, be in.

So, how to get the categories right? I recommend six steps:

- **Look up competitors online:** Use Google Maps to find local competitors and near-competitors in whatever lines of business you're involved in. Identify what categories they're listed in. Write down the category names, word for word.

- **Use the Yellow Pages:** Not only has the Yellow Pages been around for a long time, gradually adjusting its categories to fit user expectations—also, user expectations have been shaped by the many years of experience that users, especially older ones, have in using the Yellow Pages. So, use Yellow Pages categories to get ideas for words to try against Google Places categories.

- **Use industry magazines, trade shows, industry associations, and so on:** Get the names of trade magazines, trade shows, associations and so on relevant to your business, and use those as a source for keywords for categories. (Take care, though: These names are sometime "inside baseball" instead of the categories that users think in.)

▶ **Use the list at the end of this appendix:** Google has a list of category names that it makes available for volume users of Google Places. Use this list as a resource for keywords. As with trade magazines and so on, the names tend to be a bit wonky, so be sure to take the time to think like a consumer before making any final decisions.

▶ **Discuss, debate, and brainstorm:** People power can be really helpful in decisions like this one. Discuss this with people close to your business—as well as a couple who know nothing about it. Get their ideas, and listen, because it's not you who will be searching—it's ordinary people who don't know your business well.

▶ **Settle on a final list:** Narrow your list down to as few categories as possible that describe the vast majority of what your business does—but no fewer. Users like simplicity, so having just one or two categories will please them, if your business truly be described that neatly. When in doubt, use the categories competitors appear in to help you make the final decision in choosing your own.

Using the Bulk Uploading List

Google keeps a list of accepted, official category names that people who update businesses by the dozen can use. The list for the United States, as of this writing, is as follows. To find a current list for your country, visit http://www.google.com/support/places/bin/answer.py?hl=en&answer=8268 9. Use both this printed list, and the online version, as a source of ideas for keywords to use in assigning categories to your business.

Business to Business
Machine Shops
Manufacturers
Wholesalers

Education
Beauty Schools
Charter Schools
Colleges & Universities
Computer Training
Driving Schools

Elementary Schools
High Schools
Junior High Schools
Kindergartens
Middle Schools
Music Schools
Night Schools
Preschools
Private Schools
Real Estate Schools
Religious Schools
Tutoring
Vocational & Technical Schools

Entertainment
Adult
Archery Ranges
Arenas & Stadiums
Art Galleries
Athletic, Fitness, & Health Clubs
    & Gymnasiums
Auto Racing & Speedways
Ballrooms
Batting Cages
Beaches
Billiards & Pool
Bingo
Bowling
Bridge & Card Clubs
Climbing
Comedy Clubs
Country Clubs
Dance Classes
Dance Clubs
Dinner Theaters
Disc Jockeys
Driving Ranges
Football

Golf Courses
Gymnastics
Hiking
Karaoke
Live Music
Miniature Golf Courses
Movie Theaters
Museums
Night Clubs
Opera Houses
Orchestras & Symphonies
Paintball
Parks
Performing Arts Theaters &
    Playhouses
Planetariums
Racquetball Courts
Self Defense & Martial Arts
    Classes
Shooting Ranges
Skating Rinks
Ski Slopes
Soccer Clubs
Spas
Squash Courts
Swimming Pools
Tennis Courts
Tourist Attractions
Wineries
Yoga Classes

Government Offices
County
Courts
Education & School
Federal
Fire Departments
Local

Police
Post Offices
Sheriffs
State

Health and Medical
Abortion Services
Acupuncture
Alcoholism Counseling &
    Treatment
Allergists
Alternative Medicine
Animal Hospitals
Assisted Living
Cardiologists
Chiropractors
Clinics & Medical Centers
Counseling
Dentists
Dermatologists
Endocrinologists
Family & General Practice
    Physicians
Gastroenterologists
Geriatrics
Gynecologists
Hematologists
Hospices
Hospitals
Immunologists
Infectious Diseases
Infertility
Internal Medicine
Nephrology
Neurologists
Neurosurgeons
Nursing Homes
Obstetricians

Oncologists
Ophthalmologists
Optometrists
Orthodontists
Orthopedics
Otolaryngologists
Pain Management
Pediatricians
Physical Therapists
Plastic Surgeons
Podiatrists
Psychiatrists
Psychologists
Pulmonologists
Radiologists
Rheumatologists
Sports Medicine
Surgeons
Travel Medicine
Urologists
Veterinarians

Organizations
Chambers of Commerce
Charities
Churches
Fraternal
Historical Societies
Mosques
Non-Profit
Professional
Religious
Sports Clubs
Stock Exchanges
Synagogues & Temples
Volunteer
Welfare
Youth

Real Estate
Agents & Realtors
Apartment Buildings &
    Complexes
Appraisers
Commercial
Home Inspection
Property Management
Surveyors

Restaurants
Afghan
African
All You Can Eat
American
Argentinean
Australian
Austrian
Banquet Halls
Barbecue
Bars, Pubs, & Taverns
Belgian
Brazilian
Breakfast & Brunch
Breweries & Brewpubs
British
Buffets
Cafes
Cajun
Caribbean
Caterers
Chilean
Chinese
Coffee Shops
Colombian
Creole
Cuban
Czech

Delicatessens
Delivery
Dessert
Dim Sum
Diners
Ethiopian
Family Style
Fast Food
Fine Dining
French
German
Greek
Halal
Hungarian
Ice Cream
Indian
Indonesian
Irish
Italian
Jamaican
Japanese
Korean
Kosher
Lebanese
Malaysian
Mexican
Middle Eastern
Moroccan
Nepali
Pakistani
Pizza
Polish
Polynesian
Portuguese
Russian
Sandwiches
Seafood
Southern

Southwestern
Spanish
Sports Bars
Steakhouses
Sushi
Swedish
Takeout
Tapas
Thai
Tibetan
Turkish
Vegan
Vegetarian
Vietnamese

Retail Stores
Animals & Pets
Antiques & Collectibles
Appliances
Art Supplies
Automobile Alarms
Automobile Audio
Automobile Parts & Supplies
Automobiles
Automobiles—New
Automobiles—Used
Awards & Trophies
Baby Clothing & Supplies
Bakeries
Banks
Beds & Mattresses
Beer
Bicycle
Boating
Books & Magazines
Bridal
Building Supplies
Butchers

CDs, Records, & Tapes
Camera & Photography
Candles
Candy
Carpet & Flooring
Charity & Thrift
Cheese
China & Glassware
Cigars, Cigarettes, Tobacco, &
    Smoking
Clothing
Comic Books
Computers
Consignment
Convenience
Cosmetics
Costumes
Craft Supplies
Credit Unions
DVDs, Videotapes, & Movies
Department
Discount
Electrical Equipment
Electronics
Equipment Rental
Fabric, Sewing Supplies, &
    Notions
Fireplace Equipment
Fireworks
Fish & Seafood
Fishing Supplies
Flea Markets
Florists
Furniture
Games & Hobbies
Garden & Gardening
Gas Stations
Gift

Gift Baskets
Green Grocers
Grocery & Supermarkets
Guns
Hardware
Health Food
Hot Tubs, Saunas, Spas, &
    Swimming Pools
Hunting
Jewelry
Kitchen
Laundromats
Lighting
Lingerie
Liquor
Lumber
Maps
Medical Supplies
Mobile Homes
Motorcycles
Music & Musical Instruments
Newspapers
Office Equipment & Supplies
Opticians
Outdoor Furniture
Outlets
Paint, Wallpaper, & Wall Coverings
Paper
Party Supplies
Pawn Shops
Pharmacies
Plants
Plumbing Equipment & Supplies
Recreational Vehicles
Restaurant Supplies
Shoes
Shopping Centers & Malls
Skiing

Sporting Goods
State Stores
Surplus
Telephones
Theater Supplies
Tires
Toupees & Wigs
Toys
Tuxedo Rental
Video Games
Watches
Wine
Wool & Yarn

Services
Accounting
Advertising Agencies
Alteration & Tailoring
Animal Control
Animal Shelters
Animal Training
Appliance Repair
Appraisal
Arborists & Tree Services
Architects
Astrologers, Palm Readers, &
    Psychics
Attorneys
Auctions
Auto Detailing & Washing
Automobile Repair
Bail Bonds
Barbers
Beauty Salons
Body Piercing
Burglar Alarm
Cable & Satellite Television
Car Washes

Carpet Cleaning

Cemeteries

Check Cashing

Cleaning & Maid

Computer Consulting

Computer Networking

Computer Repair

Computer Security

Conference Facilities & Halls

Construction

Consulting

Convention Facilities

Copying

Courier & Delivery

Court Reports & Stenographers

Currency Exchange

Data Recovery

Dating

Day Care Centers & Nurseries

Dry Cleaning

Dumps & Landfills

E-Commerce

Electrical

Electronics Repair

Embroidery

Employment & Temporary
    Agencies

Engineering

Engraving

Event Planning

Facsimile Sending & Receiving

Family Planning

Fencing & Fence Repair

Financial Planning

Food Banks

Funeral Homes & Mortuaries

Garage Door Installation

Gardening & Landscaping

General Contractors

Glass & Window Repair

Graphic Design

Hair Removal

Handyman

Heating, Ventilation, & Air
    Conditioning

Home Remodeling & Repair

Human & Social Services

Importing & Exporting

Insurance

Interior Design

Internet Marketing

Internet Service Providers

Investments

Janitorial Services

Junkyards

Kennels

Landscape Design

Laundry

Legal Aid

Libraries

Locksmiths

Marinas

Marketing

Massage

Modeling Agencies

Mortgage Services

Moving

Music

Nail Salons

Notary Public

Painting

Passport

Personal Trainers

Pest Control

Pet Boarding

Pet Grooming

Pet Sitting
Photographers
Piano Repair & Tuning
Picture Framing
Plumbing
Pressure Washing
Printing
Process Servers
Public Relations
Publishing
Record Management & Storage
Recording Studios
Recycling
Roofing
Secretarial
Security
Self Storage
Shipping & Receiving
Shoe Repair
Siding
Signs
Skin Care
Snow Plowing & Removal
Software Development
Stables
Storage
Swimming Pool & Hot Tub
Talent Agencies
Tanning Salons
Tattooing
Tax Preparation
Telephone
Ticket Sales
Title Companies
Towing
Trash & Waste Removal
Trucking
Upholstery

Utilities
Video Production
Watch Repair
Web Design
Web Development
Web Hosting
Wedding Photographers
Wedding Planning
Welding
Window Treatments

Transportation
Airlines
Airport Shuttles
Airports
Automobile Rental
Bicycling
Boats & Ferries
Bus
Limousines
Parking Facilities
Subways
Taxicabs
Trains

Travel
Bed & Breakfasts
Camps & Campgrounds
Casinos
Cruises
Hostels
Hotels
Motels
Recreational Vehicle Parks
Tour Operators
Travel Agents
Vacation Rentals

Index